BECOMING DADS

BECOMING DADS

An Innovative Fatherhood Curriculum

PARTICIPANT GUIDE

Becoming Dads: An Innovative Fatherhood Curriculum (Participant Guide)
First Edition Trade Book, © 2021
© 2021 by Marvin Charles

All rights reserved. No part of this publication may be reproduced, stored in a retrieval system, or transmitted in any form by any means—electronic, mechanical, photocopy, recording, or otherwise—except for brief quotations in critical reviews or articles, without the prior permission of the author or publisher, except as provided by U.S. copyright law.

To contact, or to order additional books:
www.aboutdads.org

Also available on Amazon.com

ISBN: 978-1-952943-98-0

Editorial and Book Packaging: Inspira Literary Solutions, Gig Harbor, WA

Printed in the U.S.A.

Table of Contents

Divine Alternatives for Dads Services ix
Author and Instructor ....

0.0 | Course Introduction 1
0.1 Course Goal 1
0.2 Course Objectives 1
0.3 DADS Pre-survey 2

1.0 | Turning Your Life Around 5
1.1 Engage: The Role of a Dad 6
1.2 The Becoming Dads Pledge 7
1.3 The Dollar Bill Story 8
1.4 This is Your Life 10
1.6 Change 12
1.7 The Dad Plan 16

2.0 | Every Dad's Challenge: Being There 17
2.1 FatherLESSness 18
    2.1.a Want Ad for a Dad 18
    2.1.b Defining Fatherlessness 18
    2.1.c The Impact of Fatherlessness 20
2.2 FatherFULLness 21
    2.2.a What Children Say About FatherFULLness 21
    2.2.b How Research Defines FatherFULLness 22
    2.2.c What Research Says About FatherFULLness 23
2.3 A Lifetime Commitment as a Father 24
    2.3.a The Amos Story 24
    2.3.b What Being Your Child's Father Means to You 26
2.4 The Dad Plan 27

3.0 | What Men Do 29
3.1 Man Up 30
3.1.a Activity: What Kind of Man Are You? 30
3.1.b The Elephant in the Room 30
3.1.c What Do Men Do 31
3.2 Marry Up 33
3.2a Your History with Women 34
3.2.b How to Treat a Woman 37
3.3 Daddy Up 40
3.3.a What Your Child Needs 41
3.3.b What Dads Do 45
3.4 The Dad Plan 46

4.0 | Overcoming Challenges 47
4.1 Stable in Stress 48
4.1.a The Stress Test 48
4.1.b What Is Stress? 48
4.1.c The Impact of Stress 50
4.2 The Trouble with Trauma 54
4.2.a Cuts Like a Knife 54
4.2.a The ACE Study 55
4.2.b The Ace Survey 56
4.3 Healing, Forgiving, Making Amends and Moving On 60
4.3.a Dice Activity 2 Steps Forward, 3 Steps Back ... 60
4.3.b Feel Like Giving Up? 61
4.3.c Forgiveness and Moving Forward 64
4.4 The Dad Plan 66

5.0 | Becoming Dad 67
5.1 Better Relational Skills 68
5.1.a The Family Tree 68
5.1.b Family Needs 69
5.1.c Speaking 72
5.1.d Listening 73
5.2 Co-Parenting 75
5.2.a Family Sculpturing 75
5.2.b Getting Past the Drama 75

Divine Alternatives for Dads Services

Marvin Charles is the founder and executive director of Divine Alternatives for Dads Services based in Seattle, Washington. For over 20 years, he has been effectively helping men in surrounding communities reclaim their positive role as the fathers their children need. Marvin's own powerful story of separation and reunification with his family, parents and children, fueled his passion for ministry, gave him experience, and earned the trust of other men to be their mentor and advisor.

Marvin is also an emerging national leader in creating stronger fathers and healthier families. He travels across the U.S. to speak about empowering fathers, to learn from other national leaders, and to share his successes with other organizations planning to implement fatherhood programs.

Marvin is the author of Becoming Dads, which chronicles his life and the beginnings of Divine Alternatives for Dads Services. He is an ordained minister and his extraordinary effectiveness comes from his ability to see through the pain and threats of those he counsels to the powerful change possible by embracing a living God and larger purpose. Neither class nor ethnicity pose an obstacle to Marvin's being heard.

Marvin and his wife, Jeanett, have a beautiful blended family of eight children, including Dontay, Nick, Marvin Jr., Jeffrey, Lyric, Devotion, Marvette, and Jamie.

Author and Instructor

George R. Williams, Ph.D., is a trained marriage and family therapist and family life education consultant with almost two decades of experience as a curricula developer, fathering practitioner, master trainer, public speaker, and consultant, who has passionately served some of our most vulnerable citizens from all walks of life.

Dr. Williams is the Assistant Director for Faith-based and Community Initiatives for the Kansas Department for Children and Families, leading work on state-wide projects such as Mental Health Awareness, Kansas Strong Dads, Social Worker

Courses, the Kansas Community Leadership Enterprise and the Governor's Mental Health Taskforce. Prior to this, he served as the Director of Addiction and Prevention Services, responsible for all Kansas Substance Use Disorder (SUD) services—managing a staff of 23, a budget of $46 million, and oversight of 200 SUD service providers.

Dr. Williams served a decade at the National Center for Fathering as the former executive director of urban fathering developing and delivering fathering education and programming in communities across the country. As a nationally recognized fathering and family expert, he has spoken and taught at many national conferences, including the National PTA Conference, the National Welfare Reform Conference and the National Head Start Fathering Conference and has inspired and helped thousands across the country with his creative, engaging and passionate presentations and training. Dr. Williams has been featured in national media and has authored numerous fathering articles and teaching materials, including Kansas Strong Dads, Super Kids, READ to Kids, Males to MEN, Quenching the Father Thirst, and Kansas HOPE Mentoring. He is a contributing author for the book, Why Fathers Count.

Dr. Williams earned his Bachelor of Science degree in computer science and a Doctorate in family studies from Kansas State University (Manhattan, KS.) He earned his Master of Science degree from Friends University (Wichita, KS) in marriage and family therapy. He and Trudy, his wife of thirty-two years, have three sons and a daughter and live in the greater Kansas City area.

0.0 Course Introduction

0.1 Course Goal

The goal of the *Becoming Dads* curriculum is to help men in challenging situations to take increasing responsibility and action to heal and make changes necessary to become the dad their children need, so that their children can thrive and be successful for the next generation.

0.2 Course Objectives

The purpose of this curriculum is for participants to build knowledge, adjust attitudes, and apply skills related to men becoming the dads their children need. At the completion of the curriculum they will:

1. Face the truth of their past and have hope for a better future
2. Understand the impact in their role as a father
3. Know what their children need from them
4. Be committed to their children for a lifetime
5. Understand the character of a man who lives for others
6. Know how to have a healthy relationship with their child's mother
7. Start on the road to healing and getting past hurdles to effective fathering
8. Have grounding in their spiritual walk and maintenance
9. Improve their employment situation
10. Understand the child support system
11. Get on track to providing child support

0.3 DADS Pre-survey

Instructions: *Please check the box of your response.*

	5 = Strongly Agree	4 = Agree	3 = Neutral	2 = Disagree	1 = Strongly Disagree
1. I would not mind if my son grew up to be someone just like me.	❏	❏	❏	❏	❏
2. I want my daughter to marry someone like me.	❏	❏	❏	❏	❏
3. I believe that fathers are just as important as mothers.	❏	❏	❏	❏	❏
4. A father's involvement includes physical, social, emotional, and spiritual presence.	❏	❏	❏	❏	❏
5. I believe that men need help to become the fathers their children need.	❏	❏	❏	❏	❏
6. Men and women should be treated as equals in every way.	❏	❏	❏	❏	❏
7. Fathers and mothers must work together for the benefit of their child even if they are not together.	❏	❏	❏	❏	❏
8. Violence has no place in the family between mothers, fathers, and children.	❏	❏	❏	❏	❏
9. I have open communication with the mother of my child.	❏	❏	❏	❏	❏
10. My child knows that I am available for him or her night or day.	❏	❏	❏	❏	❏
11. I am responsible to take care of the physical, emotional, social, and spiritual needs of my child.	❏	❏	❏	❏	❏

12. I know where my child should be developmentally.	❏	❏	❏	❏	❏
13. I regularly express my love to my child by saying it and showing it.	❏	❏	❏	❏	❏
14. I have regular interaction with my child either by reading, playing, or talking.	❏	❏	❏	❏	❏
15. I am involved in my child's education.	❏	❏	❏	❏	❏
16. I am currently paying child support.	❏	❏	❏	❏	❏
17. I am employed or currently looking for employment.	❏	❏	❏	❏	❏
18. I have regular access to my child anytime during the day.	❏	❏	❏	❏	❏
19. I have started a college savings account for my child and am contributing monthly.	❏	❏	❏	❏	❏
20. I am attending a weekly support group to improve my fathering, spiritual well-being, or sobriety.	❏	❏	❏	❏	❏
21. During my childhood my parents were always in my life.	❏	❏	❏	❏	❏
22. I have never been incarcerated.	❏	❏	❏	❏	❏
23. I was never abused during my childhood.	❏	❏	❏	❏	❏
24. I have been sober for more than one year.	❏	❏	❏	❏	❏
25. No one in my family has a mental disorder.	❏	❏	❏	❏	❏

1.0 Turning Your Life Around

GOAL

To become a better dad
I will turn my life around
Face the truth and break free from the things,
that at one time held me down

OBJECTIVES

1. The Role of a Dad
2. The Dollar Bill Story
3. Are you ready for a change?

How widespread is father absence? A past quote from the *New York Times* (1971) says it all, "Most American children suffer too much mother and too little father." In other words, children are missing out on the full benefits of a healthy involved father. Father absence has been at an historic high in America since the 1990s and continues to impact over 25% of U.S. children.

Fathers are critically important to children—fathers are their champions and superheroes. Children want and need their fathers. "Nothing can replace a father spending time with his children." Let this be the motivation for fathers to turn their lives around and become the fathers their children need.

1.1 Engage: The Role of a Dad

Using a single sheet of paper, you can create many objects. The Japanese culture has an art form called *origami*, or the art of paper folding. There is a good chance when you were in school, you made things with paper to play with, and sometimes to pass the time. This next exercise may take you back to an early time when you created things with paper for fun.

Instructions: You will be handed a standard 8.5 x 11-inch sheet of paper. You will be given a time limit, and asked to make something out of that piece of paper. (Williams, 2010)

Process Questions

1. What did you make?
2. Why did you make it?
3. How can you compare this exercise with how you came to be the person you are today?
4. What is the implication of this exercise for us?

Instructions: Try to determine letters that complete the phrase below that summarizes our previous paper activity.

D							
A							
D							
S							!

(Williams, 2010)

1.1 Dads play a critical role in helping or hindering the success of their child.

1.2 The Becoming Dads Pledge

For any worthwhile pursuit in life, it is helpful to have a guide that will keep you on the road to success. The following is the Becoming a Better Dad Pledge, which is the road map to this curriculum.

Please keep in mind that the time you spend in this class is a direct investment in your child. As we become better men, our children benefit from a better dad.

Instructions: Read through the following pledge and answer the process questions. Be ready to discuss with the group.

Becoming a Better Dad

To become a better dad
I will turn my life around
Face the truth and break free from the things
That at one time held me down.

To become a better dad
I will commit to being there
For the sake of my child
By investing this time here.

To become a better dad
I will do what men do
Mature; respect women; love and serve others
And that includes my children too.

To become a better dad
I need healing from my past
All the hurt, trauma, and failures
Forgiving, making amends, moving forward at last.

To become a better dad
I will be humble and seek to learn
Ways to improve as a parent, co-parent, and citizen
And let this passion to be better burn.

I will become a better dad
No matter how tough I won't quit or give up
Through the support of my faith, family, and community
Until my last breath and my eyes finally shut.

Process Questions

1. Is there anything you would add, delete, or change in this pledge?
2. What is one thing in this pledge that spoke to you?
3. Is this a reasonable goal for your role as a man and father?
4. What might be some challenges to fulfilling this pledge?
5. Would you commit to fulfilling this pledge for your child?

1.2 I will "daddy up."

1.3 The Dollar Bill Story

Unfortunately, the role of the father often gets boiled down to one thing: providing. It is like every father in America has the same first name and last name. The first name is Dollar and the last name is Bill. Of course, a large part of being a father is providing, but it's not just about the money. Additionally, children need the love, support, and guidance from their mothers and fathers to help them thrive and be successful in life. Following is the story of a man and father whose first name is Bill and his struggle to be a better father.

The Dollar Bill Story

After serving four years in prison on drug-related charges, William Haynes was lucky to find employment as a sheet metal worker. At 34, the father of five children had never held a job and it felt good to be earning his own money for the first time. But, what Haynes didn't know is that child support obligations, which he said he never knew about, had been accruing even while he was incarcerated.

By the time he was released from prison in 2001, he owed $133,000, and after two months or so on the job, the state had started to garnish his pay. "They were taking practically all the money I was making," Haynes said. "I was left with maybe $75 a week. I felt like I was paying a note to a house I would never live in." It was around that time that Haynes met Marvin Charles, who had traveled a similar path in life.

Marvin and his wife, Jeanett, had taken what they had learned working with guys like Haynes, as well as working to win their own children back from the state, to create an organization that helps fathers—and a few mothers, too—navigate the murky bureaucracy around child support and parenting.

Their faith-based non-profit, Divine Alternatives for DADS Services, or DADS, is built around the belief that fathers are the cornerstone of a healthy family. Fatherlessness in this country, they say, is at the root of $100 billion in annual costs to the federal government. "It's the true breakdown of the family," Jeanett said. "Generation on top of generation—grandmothers, and aunties raising kids without a father present."

From its offices along Rainier Avenue in Seattle, DADS provides services around child support and parenting and offers counseling and education aimed at empowering men to become more responsible and accountable fathers. "There's not a man in this country who doesn't want to be his children's hero," Marvin told a Congressional subcommittee.

Back in 2001, the couple had worked alongside Haynes as he tried to get the state to modify his child support payments to fit his budget. He even eventually got the $133,000 he owed whittled down to a more manageable $11,000.

On top of that, Haynes, now 49 and married, created a parenting plan that allowed him to be a father to his children, including a reunion with his twins, a boy and a girl, who had been adopted and taken out of state while he was in prison. Two of his kids are now in college, another is in the U.S. Marine Corps Forces Reserve, and the other two are raising families of their own.

"Marvin and Jeanett take a holistic approach, helping you confront the issues that caused you to be in trouble or away from your kids in the first place," said Haynes. "They make it so a person can stand on his feet and be supportive of himself and his kids," he continued. "They don't just talk about it; they model it as well."

Process Questions

1. How do drugs interfere with being a father?
2. What impact does incarceration have on being a father?
3. How can you be a dad if you can't get a job?
4. What is the mission of the child support system?
5. What are all the things that children need from their father?
6. What kind of help do dads need?

1.3 It can be hard for a man to be a dad, but even harder for a child to be without one.

1.4 This Is Your Life

Just like William had a story, so do you. When you think back over your life, you can soon realize that certain events or experiences help shape who you are. This shaping is done by the good things that happen in your life as well as the bad. What were the bad things that happened in William's life? What were the good things that happened in William's life? In this next exercise, everyone will get an opportunity to look at their life and determine the good and bad things they experienced.

Instructions: Reflect over your life and select three good and bad experiences that may have shaped you. Describe the event, what you thought or felt through it, and how it might have shaped or influenced your life.

Good Experiences

	Event	Thought or Feeling	Action
1			
2			
3			

Bad Experiences

	Event	Thought or Feeling	Action
1			
2			
3			

Process questions:

1. Would you like to share any good experiences?
2. Would you like to share any bad experiences?
3. When you have a good or bad experience, how can you make a choice to move backward, stay there, or move forward?

1.5 When dads face tough experiences, they have a choice to move backward, stay there, or move forward.

1.6 Change

Instructions: Sign your name in the first box below. When done, please wait for the instructions from the facilitator before proceeding.

[ ]

Instructions: Next, sign your name in the second box, using your other hand.

[ ]

Process Questions

1. How did you feel when you were asked to sign your name in the box another way?
2. Did it come naturally, or did you have to stop and think about it?
3. Were you comfortable doing this differently from your normal process?
4. What are some things that make us resistant to change?

Change is not comfortable.

The concept of homeostasis is from the field of biology. The human body regulates itself to keep a steady state, or "homeostasis" (Cannon, 1932). For example, when the blood sugar is too high, the body thirsts for water in an attempt to dilute the sugar levels to return it back to equilibrium. In short, any change in the body is met with resistance and an attempt to change it back.

This concept is also used in family therapy. The idea is that families and individuals resist change in order to maintain the steady state. This is what keeps families and individuals stuck in cycles or certain behaviors. It is like a car getting stuck in a rut. The car wheel is trying to roll forward, but cannot get the momentum to break free, so it rolls right back into the rut.

Seligman and Maier (1967) conducted classical conditioning research, in which dogs associated a shock with another stimulus and exhibited learned helplessness. A similar experiment was repeated for humans using loud sounds instead of shocks that resulted in similar outcomes. We must consider the experiences that people go through and learn how it shapes them and their responses of what they do. Some people have learned to be helpless and it is not easy to change.

Process Questions

1. What do you think about the following statement: "Change is not always natural or easy, but it is often necessary."?
2. What are some examples of changes you have tried to make, but have found difficult?

**Change is not easy and, when we try to change,
we often change back to our old patterns.**

The Stages of Change Model is widely used in the field of addiction counseling as a way to understand how people are motivated to change. There are five stages that people cycle through several times before they actually make a change (Prochaska, DiClemente and Norcross, 1992).

Stages of Change Model
Prochaska, 1992

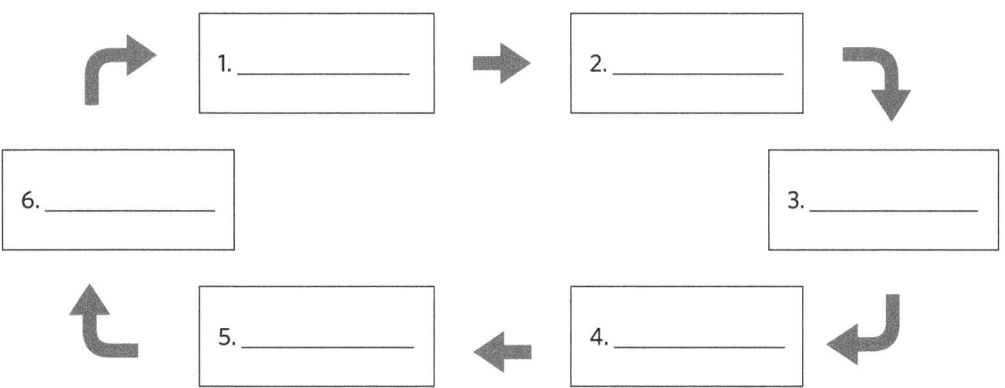

Instructions: Fill in the stages in the diagram using the following definitions to match following words: (Maintenance, Preparation, Relapse, Pre-contemplation, Action, Contemplation).

1. The dad does not see a need to change right now.
2. The dad sees a need for change and is thinking about changing.
3. The dad intends to take action in the near future.
4. The dad makes changes in behavior.
5. The dad needs to sustain the change and not slip back into the rut.
6. The dad starts again with the change.

1.6 The success or failure (feedback) of a person making a change is based on stages of change and the strength of the motivation for the change.

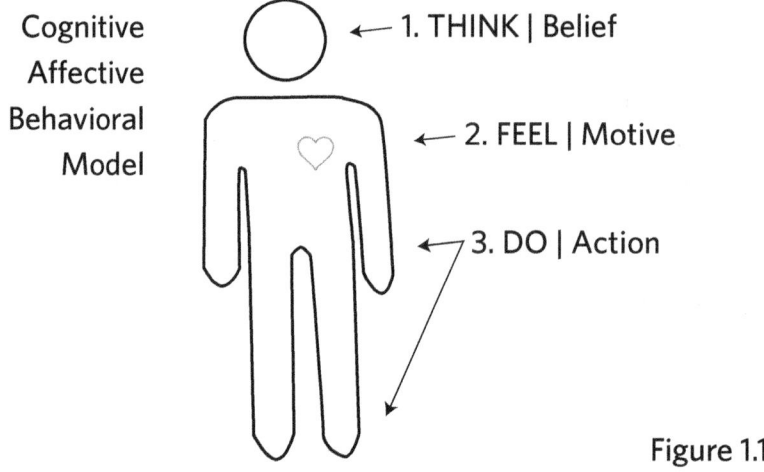

Figure 1.1

One aid to help visualize making a change is the idea of "turning our life around." It is making a 180-degree turn. This idea is summarized in the concept of repentance. It is turning from one way and turning to another way. How do we begin to make a change?

The Better Dad Model can help guide our change. The model is about aligning what you think, feel, and do to become a better dad for your child. In this section, we will write out a core belief, a passion, and an action that will help guide and motivate us to be a better dad. The following is an example of this model:

Example:

1. My main belief (think) is that a father is responsible for his child.
2. My motivation (feel) is my child's life is more important than my own.
3. My change (do) is to help my child grow and develop.

Instructions: Write down your main belief, motivation, and change that will help make you a better dad.

1. What is your main belief?

   _____
   _____
   _____
   _____

2. What is your motivation?

   _____
   _____
   _____
   _____

3. What is your change?

   _____
   _____
   _____
   _____

1.7 The Dad Plan

Fathering Skill: Become a better dad by turning my life around.

Instructions: Answer the following questions to create your dad plan to become a better dad.

1. What is my specific SMART (Specific, Measurable, Achievable, Realistic, Timetable) goal for turning my life around?
2. What can I do every day this week to grow more culturally aware?
3. When and where will I do this?
4. Who will hold me accountable?

2.0 Every Dad's Challenge: Being There

GOAL

To become a better dad
I will commit to being there
For the sake of my child
By investing this time here.

OBJECTIVES

1. Fatherlessness
2. Fatherfulness
3. A lifetime commitment as a father, not a life sentence without one

Commitment is a verb—an action word. Commitment is a pledge to do something. Helping our child develop in every way requires the commitment of being there. Fathering is rewarding, but also requires some hard work. And without commitment, hard work does not get done.

We need to resolve to be the father who is there for his children. To overcome any barriers to fathering a man must have a strong commitment. How strong is your commitment to your children? You may say you are willing to die for your children, but are you willing to daily live for them, no matter what you face? Our commitment should be in words and deeds.

2.1 FatherLESSness

2.1.a Want Ad for a Dad

Instructions: Imagine being an eight-year old child again and you don't have a father. What would you want in a father? Take two minutes to write a want ad for the type of dad you would want from a child's perspective. Include the duties, salary, and benefits of being your father (Williams, 2010).

Process Questions:

1. Why did you write what you wrote?
2. What does your ad say about you?
3. Could you answer your own ad?
4. What do you think your child would write?

2.1.b Defining Fatherlessness

Traditionally, when we hear about absent fathers, we relate it to fathers that are physically absent. However, a father can be absent in other ways, such as, socially, emotionally, morally, and/or spiritually. A father can live in the home (physically present), but he may also be absent socially and emotionally.

Father absence can be a permanent or temporary state in which systemic or personal barriers and/or choices prevent a father from providing his resources or social capital to his child. Examples of systemic barriers that make it difficult or impossible for the father to be involved in his child's life include: incarceration (wrongful), war, severe mental or physical disability, a hostile divorce or separation, or death.

Fathers can also make personal choices that prevent their involvement. Some choices that lead to personal barriers of involvement include addiction, lack of physical and mental health maintenance, risky behaviors, irresponsibility, abandonment, crime, career choices, child abuse and neglect, and incarceration. It is possible the reason for the absence may lessen aspects of the impact on the child; however, the results are the same no matter the circumstances and that is the forfeiture of the provision of social capital for the child.

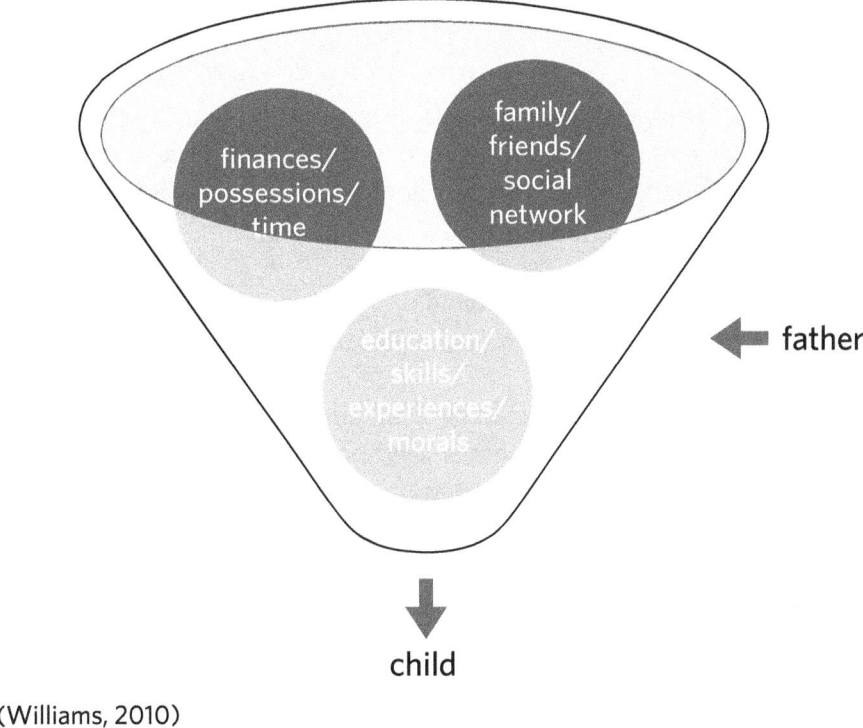

(Williams, 2010)

A father absence is when a father—through barriers or personal choice—abandons providing the resources or support physically, mentally, socially, emotionally, financially, and/or spiritually for his child.

Process Questions:
1. What are some of the other things a father provides for his child?
2. What are some examples of physical, mental, social, emotional, financial, and spiritual absence?

2.1.c The Impact of Fatherlessness

Father absence in the U.S. is widespread. There is not a one-to-one relationship between fathers living absent from their biological children and father involvement. Many of these fathers manage to stay involved in the lives of their children. However, the opposite is also true, that fathers can be present in the home and absent other ways.

1. The four ways a father can be absent are P_____, E_____, S_____, and M_____.

Princeton sociologist Sara McLanahan, a single mother, set out to prove that single motherhood did not negatively impact the well-being of children. The more she investigated, the more evidence she found that supported the opposite conclusion (McLanahan & Sandefur, 1994).

2. Children in single mother families fared p_____ across a wide range of outcomes including: financial, emotional, behavioral, legal, and sexual.

Childhood poverty in America is affected by a father's absence in the family. Less than a third of children living in two-parent homes lived below the poverty level, while 70% of children living in single-mother families lived below the poverty level in 2009 (Mather, 2010). Poverty can be viewed as an accelerator to many other outcomes, because of the inherent lack of support and resources of this condition. Also, there is a chance of a repeating generational cycle.

Following is a list of other research findings of the negative impact of father absence on the outcome of children:

- When fathers are absent, their children are at higher risk of suffering from negative outcomes including: emotional and behavioral problems, poverty, child abuse and neglect, substance abuse, low educational attainment, and teen pregnancy (McLanahan & Sandefur, 1994; Angel & Angel, 1996; Mott, Kowaleski-Jones, & Menaghen, 1997; Hoffmann & Johnson, 1998; Brown, Cohen, Johnson, & Salzinger, 1998).
- Data from the National Longitudinal Survey of Youth indicated that a father's absence significantly increased by two times the likelihood of difficulties with peers, depressive behavior in boys, and other behavioral challenges for girls (Mott, 1993).

- A population-based survey study that included one million children, revealed that children from single-parent homes were at twice the risk for mental disorders, suicide and attempted suicide, and alcohol or drug abuse compared to two-parent families (Weitoft, Hjern, Haglund, & Rosen, 2003).
- Students living in father-absent homes were twice as likely to repeat a grade and 1.7 times more likely to drop out of high school than children living with both parents (McNeal, 1995; Nord & West, 2001).
- My research study on non-intact families found that the lower the quantity and quality of biological father involvement during childhood, the lower the level of adult child education, employment, income, physical health, social attainment, sobriety, sexual fidelity, parental success, paternal closeness, and happiness (Williams, 2016).

2. Willful father absence is a form of C_____ A_____ and N_____ (Williams, 2010).

2.1 The result of father absence places his child at a higher risk for many negative outcomes.

Process Questions:
1. What do you think about fathers who are absent?
2. What is the impact on the children?
3. Have you been absent in the life of your child?

2.2 FatherFULLness

2.2.a What Children Say about FatherFULLness

Since 1992, the National Center for Fathering has collected over 1,000,000 essays written by kindergarten through twelfth grade students describing what their father or father figure means to them. One interesting finding in these essays is that, even in the cases where children have written about absent or "bad" fathers, they would still share they needed them. The children would describe the hurt caused by their father's absence or poor fathering, but finish with something like, "I still want him to know I love him and need him." The following is an example of a typical positive essay, written by a first grader.

My father is the best.
My dad helps me when I'm hurt.
He plays with me a lot.
He makes breakfast for my family.
He lets me have friends over.
My dad helps me ride my bike.
When he gets home, we turn on a movie and cuddle. We cuddle with each other a lot.
He plays soccer with me.
He helps me do my math.
He helps me read.
My dad was the second person who held me when I was just born.
My dad is in the Air Force and he saves our country.
My dad is a very good dad.
Thank you, Dad, for being my hero and my dad.
I love you.
(National Center for Fathering, 2015)

Process Questions:

1. Is there anything in this child's essay that stands out to you?
2. Why would children still have a place in their heart for absent dads?

2.2.b How Research Defines FatherFULLness

Examining further the importance of the role of the father requires exploring what fathers do, why and when they do it and how might it make a difference for children. One of the most researched concepts when it comes to the roles of fathers is involvement (Williams, 2016).

Outside of the realm of biology, fatherhood is a social construct that defines a father's involvement with his child. The construct of fatherhood has transitioned over time throughout American history from a role with the main emphasis on a father's participation as a moral teacher, household provider, and nurturing father (Williams). These one-dimensional constructs of fatherhood are descriptive of the ways fathers, during historical time periods, were expected to be involved with their children (Williams).

The concept of father involvement has evolved to explain the many diverse ways fathers, in different circumstances and situations, interact to positively influence the outcomes of their children. Accessibility, involvement, and responsibility are three basic components that have become universal to most definitions of father involvement (Williams). These components can be framed as society's perception of what children need from fathers (responsibility), how available the fathers are to meet their children's needs (accessibility), and how responsive fathers are to the needs of their children (engagement).

A father provides essential **AIR** for his children.

1. A father is A_____ by being there or available to be reached by his child.
2. A father is I_____ by being engaged in every part of his child's life.
3. A father is R_____ to meet the needs of his child.
   (Williams, 2010)

2.2 A father provides AIR (Accessibility, Involvement, and Responsibility) to help meet the physical, social, emotional, and spiritual needs of children.

2.2.c What Research Says About FatherFULLness

Here are some of the studies that confirm Rohner and Veneziano's findings documenting the positive benefits fathers bring to their children socially, behaviorally, and academically:

- A study on empathy in adulthood found that the strongest predictor of empathy for others (men and women) was the level of care and support by fathers in childhood (Koestner & Weinberger, 1990).
- Another series of investigations reported higher levels of self-control and fewer behavioral problems in school children with involved fathers (Amato & Rivera, 1999). In addition, these children were found to have higher levels of social skills, self-esteem and general life skills (Amato & Rivera).
- Data from the National Study of Families and Households showed when fathers were positively involved, children experienced fewer behavior problems and anxieties, got along better with others, and were more responsible (Mosely & Thomson, 1995).
- Summarizing an early study on a father's influence on young children, researchers indicated that a father's interest and involvement in the early years was strongly associated with higher cognitive functioning and greater academic achievement among school-age children (Biller & Kimpton, 1997).

- A Department of Education study found that children whose fathers were highly involved in their schools were more likely to do well academically, enjoy school, participate in extracurricular activities and were less likely to repeat a grade or be expelled out of school than children whose fathers were not involved (Nord & West, 2001).
- One research study on non-intact families found the higher the quantity and quality of biological father involvement during childhood, the higher the level of adult child education, employment, income, physical health, social attainment, sobriety, sexual fidelity, parental success, paternal closeness, and happiness (Williams, 2016).

2.3 A Lifetime Commitment as a Father

2.3.a The Amos Story

THE AMOS STORY

Amos left the hot cotton fields with rocks in his stomach. Earlier in the day, Clete, a house slave, had overheard a conversation between the plantation master and another man about how much money Amos should bring at the auction the next day, and he immediately told Amos.

Amos was a hard-working slave. He never complained about the long, hard, hot hours in the sun. He always met his daily quota for picking cotton, and he often helped the other slaves with their quota as well. By most plantation master's standards, Amos was an ideal slave. He should bring a nice bundle to the slave master.

Amos and Beulah had seven children. Being sold, and the splitting up of the family, was always a grim possibility. But the sudden reality for Amos and Beulah was horrifying. They made great effort not to show the children their fear and anguish as they had supper and prepared the one-room shanty for the night's rest.

Amos and his three sons unfolded the handmade blankets and placed them as pallets in their usual places on the dirt floor. Beulah brushed and plaited the hair of the four little girls. When they were ready for bed, Amos gathered the family around him and quoted by memory, because he could not read, the first verse of Psalm 23, "De Lord is my shepherd. I shall not want." Then he prayed for the family and for their rest. He even prayed for the slave master and his family. His prayer was short tonight. He wanted to stay in control of his emotions. Yet, in his heart, he was in great turmoil.

Beulah blew out the candle at the end of the small room where the children lay waiting to fall off to sleep. The children did not suspect the horrifying situation facing their mother and father. Almost in unison, they said, "Ga-nite, Momma. Ga-nite, Daddy."

In the dimly lit part of the other half of the room, near the only door, Amos held Beulah tight. He kissed her on the forehead and whispered in her ear, "I'm goin' out fer while." Knowing Amos like she did, Beulah felt he probably wanted to go pray. "Git cha some rest," he whispered as he opened the door to go out.

Amos found a spot he had used many times, back in the far corner of the big barn. There was a pile of hay there. He fell immediately on the pile and wept bitterly. He had held back his emotions since early morning, when Clete had told him about the master's plan. He had cut his prayer time short with his family, because this flood was just behind the dam. His heart was broken. The pain was unbearable. Beulah and the seven children were his life. It was his dream that if he worked hard and pleased the master, his children might earn special privileges and be pulled from the harsh conditions of the cotton fields to learn trades on the plantation, and especially learn to read. Many nights in this very spot he had prayed that they would all stay together as a family. Now his dream was about to be shattered. It was as if a jagged-edged knife was being ripped through his heart.

After what seemed like hours of sobbing, Amos sat up and began to think about his options. Clete had urged him to run away in the night. Amos had considered that option much of the day, but he could not assure himself that this was the safest option for a runaway slave. And, should he remain alive and make it to the North, he was not comforted that he and his family could be reunited one day.

As the seconds and minutes crept closer to the dreaded dawn, Amos thrashed around on the dirt ground and the pile of hay. No doubt the animals in the barn spent a sleepless night as well. They couldn't see Amos, but they could certainly hear him plead with God for help.

Soon, the early light of day began to peer through the cracks in the old barn. The roosters crowed. Amos knew his fate was before him. In a stupor, he gathered himself up. He opened the door of the barn and walked behind the barn to the lumber pile. He sat on a large tree stump. He placed his left arm on a nearby anvil. He raised his right arm high in the air. Without a single moment's hesitation, he slammed the hatchet he was holding down on his left arm. A deep, raw scream ripped out of his belly that could be heard throughout the slave quarters. In the woodpile, at his feet, lay a bloody hatchet and his left hand and wrist: the cost of a daddy to keep a slave family together.

Within minutes of that blood curdling scream, several of the slave men rushed to the back of the barn. Beulah sat up from her near sleepless night on her pallet. She knew that scream belonged to Amos. She told their oldest son to help the children get dressed while she went to the barn. She ran out the door and met other slaves running behind the barn. There she pushed her way through the emotional crowd to see Amos holding his severed left arm. There was blood everywhere. Beulah gasped at the sight. But, the horror of the scene quickly turned to bittersweet emotions for her, because she knew immediately that Amos would no longer be considered for the slave auction later that day. No master would want a mutilated slave "boy."
(Genovese, 1976).

Process Questions:

1. What stood out to you in this story?
2. What can we learn from Amos?
3. How can you apply this to your own life?

2.3.b What Being Your Child's Father Means to You

Commitment Letter

Instructions: Write a letter to your child or draw a picture that expresses your commitment. The letter is suggested to be 300 words or less (which would be about one page or three paragraphs). You can have the letter mailed to your child to make the experience more memorable.

2.4 The Dad Plan

Fathering Skill: Become a better dad; I commit to being there.

Instructions: Answer the following questions to create your dad plan to become a better dad.

1. What is my specific SMART (Specific, Measurable, Achievable, Realistic, Timetable) goal for growing in cultural awareness?
2. What can I do every day this week to grow more culturally aware?
3. When and where will I do this?
4. Who will hold me accountable?

3.0 What Men Do

GOAL

To become a better dad
I will do what men do:
Mature, respect women, love and serve others
And that includes my children too.

OBJECTIVES

1. Man Up
2. Marry Up
3. Daddy Up

When did you become a man? As I have asked men through the years, I have noticed a perplexing look on many faces. Many of these men have never been asked this question, so they have not given the subject much thought. The answers vary from taking responsibility for one's self to procreation. Noticeably absent from most responses are the character requirements of a man.

Manhood is an assisted journey of maturity and service in respect, responsibility, and righteousness in all his relationships. When a man learns his role, he is positioned to achieve his mission for life, because this man knows who he is and what his purpose is in life. We don't have to have "arrived" to be a dad, but we must be on the journey. Walking through the door of manhood, we leave behind our boyish ways. We cannot lead our sons in a journey we have never begun, and that is why it takes a man to be a dad!

3.1 Man Up

Instructions: Most people recognize the symbol for a man. While that may not be hard, the real challenge is determining this: what are the two objects that make up the symbol for men?

3.1.a Activity: What Kind of Man Are You?

Instructions: Take your place in the circle on the paper or in the chair. On three, we will ask the person in the middle, "What kind of person are you?" He will reply with any type of characteristic of a man (e.g. I am a man loves his family). If that characteristic does not apply to you, stay put. If it does apply to you, then you must move from the chair or paper to a different one. The last person in the middle who does not have a chair or paper is the next person to be asked, "What type of man are you?"

Process Questions:

1. When did you become a man?
2. What are the ingredients for being a man?
3. Who prepares you to be a man?
4. Can a woman teach a boy to be a man?

3.1.b The Elephant in the Room

Show the Delinquent Elephants Video

Process Questions:

1. What stands out to you about this video?
2. How can you compare this video to the pathway for boys to become men?
3. What do immature males do?
4. What is the main goal of being a man?
5. What is standing in the way of male maturing?

3.1.c What do men do

Instructions: Solve the crossword puzzle. Use the words to fill in the blanks to complete the definition of manhood.

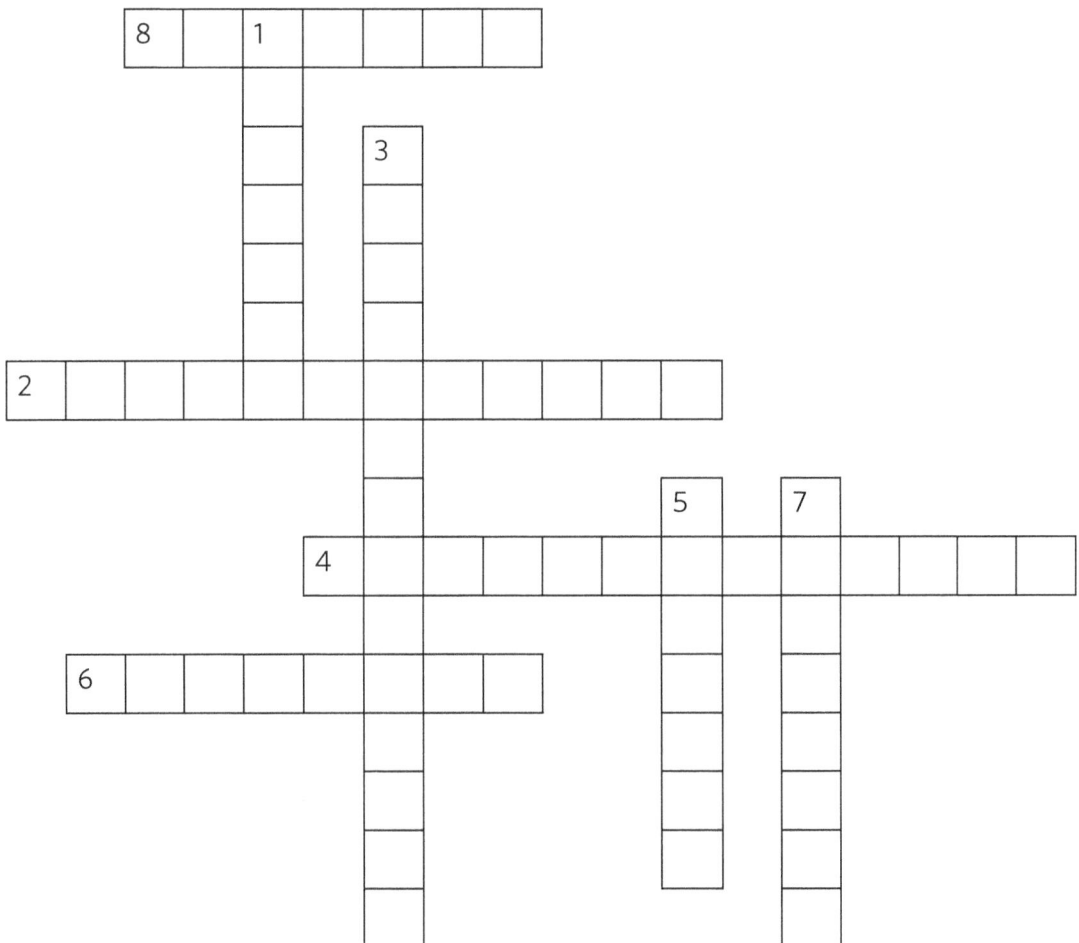

Down	Across
1. Showing value and worth for others	2. Our social connections to others
3. Owning your words and actions	4. Doing the right thing at the right time
5. A pathway to a goal destination	6. A state of growth and development
7. Someone helps you	8. When you help others

Manhood is an 7. _____ 5. _____ of 6. _____ and 8. _____ in 1. _____, 3. _____ and 4. _____ in all his 2. _____.

Process Questions:

1. Can we become a man on our own?
2. What is the journey of manhood?
3. What does a mature man look like?
4. How can we be a man for others?
5. To whom should respect be given?
6. What does it mean to be responsible?
7. Why is righteousness important in a man's life?
8. What are the different types of a man's relationships?

Assisted: We need assistance or help to become men. It should start with our fathers and continues with our sons (and daughters for womanhood).

Journey: Manhood is more of a journey or process, rather than a destination.

Maturity: You were a child and now, as a man, you put childish things behind you.

Service: When we were babies, others served us; when we were boys, we served ourselves. As men, we now serve others.

Respect: All my relationships start with respect or valuing myself and others in what I think, feel, say, and do.

Responsibility: Being responsible is taking ownership for what we do and say and for possessions.

Righteousness: Is doing the right thing, at the right time, for the right reasons.

Relationship: Part of our main purpose is to socially connect to others, which holds the key to our life, growth, and future.

Instructions: From this section, describe one thing you would like to improve on in your journey of manhood.

_____

_____

_____

_____

_____

3.2 Marry Up

Instructions: Most people recognize that this symbol represents women. While that may not be hard, the real challenge is determining this: what are the two objects that make up the symbol for a woman?

3.2a Your History with Women

A Good Woman Is Hard to Find

Instructions: Take a minute to write a list of your top five qualities of a good woman.

1. _____
2. _____
3. _____
4. _____
5. _____

Process Questions:

1. How many of these qualities are true of you?
2. Do you have to be a good man to find a good woman?
3. What can we learn from this exercise?

Relationship Foundation with Women

Instruct: Fill in the blank.

Your mother can s_____ how you relate to women.

Attachment to Your Mom

The ability for people to trust is rooted in the early relationship with their mother as a primary caregiver. This attachment is a deep and enduring emotional bond that connects one person to another. The theory on attachment provides an explanation of how the parent-child relationship emerges and influences subsequent development and future relationships (Bowlby, 1969).

If during the first three months of their children's lives, the mothers were responsive to their child's needs, then the child became securely attached and more trusting in future adult relationships. When the attachment is secure, the individual sees himself/herself as lovable and others as reliable and responsive to his/her needs. It is easy to trust.

If mothers were not responsive, then the child became insecurely or anxiously attached. Insecurely and anxiously attached individuals question whether they are lovable and whether others are reliable and responsive to their needs. It is hard for them to trust.

Instruct: Fill in the blank from the information above.

A securely attached person sees himself as L_____ and others as R_____ and R_____ to his needs.

Process Question: How can being insecurely attached cause problems in your relationships with women?

Mothering Styles

Parts of the following have been adapted from Dr. Susan Forward's 2002 book, *The Men Who Hate Women and the Women that Love Them*, published by Bantam Books.

The primary bond in a family is between the father and mother. When the father is missing, the primary bond becomes that of the mother-child. From this primary bond, unhealthy functioning in future relationships with women can result for the son if it is not properly balanced. We will refer to these bonds as different mothering styles. The mother's own fear or attempt to protect her child usually motivates these mothering styles.

The first is the over-close mothering style. This mother may inadvertently prevent her son's maturity. She does everything for him, but never cuts the umbilical cord that connects the two of them. The mother's motivation for this style is that the son may have taken the place of the absent father in the mother-father relationship. This can be seen in men who continue to stay with mothers as adults, or mothers who interfere in the relationship with the man's wife or significant other. When he gets in a relationship with another woman, he may look for a mother rather than a wife. He may choose his mother over his wife.

A second style is the over-controlling mother. This type of mothering can create resentment in the son. This mother may be overcompensating for her son's lack of a father. She wants the best for her son, but is excessively controlling in accomplishing it. She controls by being involved in too much detail, a critical attitude or any type of abuse. This can create a foundation of resentment in relationships with women that result in a power struggle. He attempts to use manipulation, abuse or hatred to have the upper hand as he relates to women.

The third is the under-emotional mothering style. In this style, the mother has experienced victimization or rejects her son. This can create an intensive need to be mothered. This can be expressed through a man's excessive sex drive, or the use of abuse to cover his vulnerability.*

Because mothers are important to children, and men need women as well, we must learn how to have respectable relationships with women. Understanding women, and how your relationship with your mother can impact how you relate to women, is important. This can help us to have healthy relationships with all the women in our lives.

Instruct: Fill in the blank from the information above.

Mothers who are over-close, over-controlling, or not available can adversely impact a son's A_____ towards women.

Process Questions:

1. What kind of relationship did you have with your mother?
2. Was there something from this reading that spoke to you?
3. What has your relationships with women been like?
4. How can you apply what you learn to your relationships with women?

Instructions: From this section, describe one thing you would like to improve in your relationship with women.

_____

_____

_____

_____

_____

---

*Susan Forward, *Men who Hate Women & The Women Who Love Them*, Bantam Books, 1987

3.2.b How to Treat a Woman

Relate To Her

In Shaunti Feldhahn's book (2006), *For Men Only*, she shares six key findings, based on a national scientific study to give men the tools they need to love their wives the way they need to be loved.

Instructions: Read the corresponding statement below and determine the word to insert into the blank to complete the statement.
(Word Bank: Enjoy, Time, Affirm, Listen, Emotionally, Reassure)

1. R_____ her often of your love.
2. E_____ understand her to be a relief value.
3. L_____ to be a filter first and a fixer later.
4. A_____ her beauty as her mirror.
5. T_____ spent just being together.
6. E_____ the relationship and the differences.

1. Many things women do that frustrate men are often signals women need to be reassured that they are loved. The marriage deal is never really closed in her life after the ceremony. It is as if your wedding vows of "I do" means to her an on-going, "Do you?" Share your love for her often.
2. Women may encounter frequent pop-ups of unresolved emotions and issues from the present and the past. When she has too much to carry, and becomes overloaded and overwhelmed, she may need a venue to share what she feels. Men may need to learn to be comfortable with emotions, because she needs you.
3. Women first want men to listen and validate how they feel about a problem before trying to fix it. Men often aren't aware of the need to take time to evaluate if the problem is emotional, and they immediately jump into fix-it mode. However, the emotion women experience is the real issue. They want those feelings to be heard and understood more than they want the problem solved.
4. In most women, the little girl is still alive and well in them, and she needs to know her man thinks she's beautiful. Women are concerned about this every day even subconsciously. A husband is a personal mirror that can choose to reflect to his wife the words of affirmation she's longing to hear. If we fail to do this, it leaves her in a fragile state, open to her own doubts and outside pressure from a hostile world. We can be a mirror or a hammer that can destroy everything.

5. Make one-on-one time together a priority. Make sure she knows you care for her first. You don't need to spend every minute outside of work with your wife, but make it clear that time together is a big priority to you. Show and share your commitment that you are there for her, no matter what. Staying away long hours to provide doesn't cut it when it hurts the very family for whom you are trying to provide. Be true partners in what goes on at home.
6. Enjoy knowing one of the most important things women wanted their men to know was overwhelmingly, "You are my hero." They expressed how much they admired, respected, and loved their husbands and wanted to make them happy. Many said how thankful they were for their wonderful husbands. In short, these women wanted their husbands to know they viewed their husbands as heroes. Nine out of ten women jumped at the chance to show how much they truly respect and appreciate their men. Enjoy your life with her.

Instructions: From this section, describe one thing you can focus on doing more to fill your significant other's emotional tank.

_____

_____

_____

_____

_____

Learn Her LOVE Language

Instructions: In the book *The Five Love Languages* (2015), Gary Chapman shares ways you can fill your spouse's emotional love tank by speaking her specific love language. Match by drawing a line between the love language and description.

1. Words of Affirmation Nothing says, "I love you," like full, undivided attention. Being there for this type of person is critical, but really being there and putting everything else on hold makes your significant other feel truly special and loved. Distractions, postponed dates, or the failure to listen can be especially hurtful.

2. Acts of Service This language isn't all about the bedroom. Hugs, pats on the back, holding hands, and thoughtful touches on the arm, shoulder, or face—they can all be ways to show excitement, concern, care, and love. Physical presence and accessibility are crucial, while neglect or abuse can be unforgivable and destructive.

3. Receiving Gifts Actions don't always speak louder than words. If this is your love language, unsolicited compliments mean the world to you. Hearing the words, "I love you," is important—hearing the reasons behind that love sends your spirits skyward. Insults can leave you shattered and are not easily forgotten.

4. Quality Time Can vacuuming the floors really be an expression of love? Absolutely! Anything you do to ease the burden of responsibilities weighing on an "Acts of Service" person will speak volumes. The words he or she most wants to hear are: "Let me do that for you." Laziness, broken commitments, and making more work for them tell speakers of this language their feelings don't matter.

5. Physical Touch Don't mistake this love language for materialism; the receiver of gifts thrives on the love, thoughtfulness, and effort behind the gift. If you speak this language, the perfect gift or gesture shows that you are known, you are cared for, and you are prized above whatever was sacrificed to bring the gift to you. A missed birthday, anniversary, or a hasty, thoughtless gift would be disastrous—so would the absence of everyday gestures.

How do you determine your love language?

The following information can help you determine your love language.

1. Your upbringing can speak into your love language. How did your parents show you love growing up? What made you feel the most loved as a child? There is a high probability that is your primary love language.
2. When you really want to show someone you care about them, what first comes to your mind to show it? Your most basic instincts can show your primary love language as well.
3. Painful relational experiences can show your primary love language. If someone close to you hurt you in a deep way or neglected to show love the way you wanted, perhaps the deep hurt/dissatisfaction came because the way you most feel loved was not met. This means that what they failed to do is what you value the most, because it is your primary love language

Instructions: From this section, describe what is your significant other's love language and share an example of why you think it fits.

_____

_____

_____

_____

_____

3.3 Daddy Up

The role of a father is ultimately defined by the child. It is all about what a father does to promote the well-being of his child. Defining child well-being includes different areas of development and need (Pollard & Lee, 2003). There are five areas of well-being that come from the research literature: 1) physical, 2) emotional, 3) social, 4) cognitive, and 5) economic (Pollard & Lee, 2003; Lippman, 2007; Bzostek, 2008). We will use these as we explore what children need and what dads do to fill those needs.

3.3.a What your child needs

Instructions: Choose from the following list to fill in the blanks.

Word Bank: [support, steer, security, survival]

1. Your child's physical needs involve their body and are critical to their _____ and growth.
2. Your child's emotional needs involve their feelings and are vital for their sense of _____ and belonging.
3. Your child's social needs involve their relationships and help strengthen their connections and _____ from others.
4. Your child's moral needs involve their behavior and _____ the choices they make in their conduct.

Instructions: Write down one example of physical, emotional, social, and moral need.

_____

_____

_____

_____

We need to be aware of our children's constant development. Their needs are also constantly changing, because of their growth. What was true of them last week may not be true of them this week.

Following is a beginning list of the types of needs and considerations we need to be aware of for our children. Our children have physical, cognitive, social, and emotional needs, along with milestones and problems to which we need to pay attention.

Instructions: Read through the developmental stages. Particularly take note of the stage your child or children are in, and their related needs, milestones, and potential problems.

Infants and Toddlers

Physical

- Provide adequate nutrition, health care, and play with your child

Cognitive

- Interact with your child by holding them, giving them face time
- Back and forth responding to what they do and say

Social

- Spend time playing, reading, talking, and taking care of them

Emotional

- Help form a secure attachment by being responsive to your child's needs and comforting them

Milestones

- Walking, talking, a mostly stable temperament, and getting along with other children

Potential Problems

- Malnutrition, lack of health care, rough treatment, lack of interaction and talking to them

Preschool

Physical

- Weight gain and height growth, gross and fine motor skills

Cognitive

- Need to grow in vocabulary, read many books

Social
- Cooperate with others and follow rules, know good from bad, exercise self-control

Emotional
- Self-esteem based on what others tell him or her; less emotional outbursts; self-directed activities

Milestones
- Toilet-trained

Potential Problems
- Social immaturity, anxiety or fear problems, lack of self-esteem or self-control, excessive aggression or tantrums, poor bladder control

School Age

Physical
- Slow, steady growth: three to four inches per year

Cognitive
- Recognize the perspective of others and the difference between behavior and intent

Social
- Friendships are situation-specific, beginning to understand social roles and taking on more responsibilities at home

Emotional
- Self-esteem

Milestones
- Puberty begins from ages 10 to 12

Potential Problems

- Emotional disturbances: depression, anxiety, PTSD, trust issues, abuse and neglect, bullying, experimentation with drugs and sex

Adolescents

Physical

- Growth spurt, puberty, body adjusting to growth spurt

Cognitive

- Can consider the consequences of thoughts and actions without experiencing them, considers the perspective of others, growth in thought and problem-solving

Social

- Distant from parents, identifying more with peer group than parents; more independent

Emotional

- More self-conscience, Developing and struggling with their own identity

Milestones

- Driving

Potential Problems

- Problems that can accompany school age: emotional disturbances: depression, anxiety, PTSD, trust issues, abuse and neglect, bullying, experimentation with drugs and sex

(Adapted from Rycus, 1998)

Instructions: Write down the needs you want to remember for your child, what they have been able to accomplish, and potential problems for which to be watchful.

_____

_____

_____

_____

_____

3.3.b What Dads Do

Men and women share many similarities and differences. While it may look different, women nurture and so do men. Nurturing is an important part of being a dad.

Children are love and care dependent. Just like a plant needs food, sun, soil, and water to grow and thrive, our children need to be nurtured. Fathers help provide the nurture children need to grow and thrive.

Instructions: Using the following word bank to fill in the blanks.
(Time, Develop, Effort, Provide, Discipline, Children, Protect, Support)

1. Nurturing is P_____ for a child's needs, P_____ a child from harm, D_____ a child with healthy boundaries and S_____ a child to develop a healthy self-image.
2. Nurturing requires T_____ and E_____.
3. According to the research, nurturing is one of the most important variables in raising a healthy C_____.
4. Nurtured children D_____ to be competent, responsible, independent, confident, achievement-oriented, and able to control aggression and become healthy adults.

3.4 The Dad Plan

Fathering Skill: Become a better dad by maturing as a man who respects women and serves others.

Remember to use SMART goals for your plan to turn your life around.

Instructions: Answer the following questions to create your dad plan to become a better dad.

1. What is my specific SMART (Specific, Measurable, Achievable, Realistic, Timetable) goal for growing in cultural awareness?
2. What can I do every day this week to grow more culturally aware?
3. When and where will I do this?
4. Who will hold me accountable?

4.0 Overcoming Challenges

Warning, this section could be a trigger for some who have experienced first or second-hand trauma. Please feel free to take a break from the group if you need to, and make sure you take care of yourself today.

GOAL

To become a better dad
I need healing from my past
All the hurt, trauma, and failures
Forgiving, making amends, moving forward at last.

OBJECTIVES

1. Stable in stress
2. The trouble with trauma
3. Healing through forgiving, making amends, and moving on

The true measure of a father's desire for his children is noting what he allows to stop him from being a dad. The road of fatherhood has many obstacles that can get in the way of fathering our children. It takes a determined man to press through these challenges and be the dad his child needs.

Another way to look at the challenges in life is that they are stressors. A stressor is a pressure we experience when we cannot cope with the demands of life.* These stressors divert our attention away from the task of being a dad in order to deal with the stress. Our

---

*Elliot Aronson, *Social Psychology*, Addison-Wesley Educational publishers Inc., 1997, p G-10

time and effort are consumed by trying to relieve the stress. Often, because of the pressure, we can be pushed to make bad decisions in handling it.

4.1 Stable in Stress

Research shows the importance of stability in a child's environment and relationships. This is especially true for the relationship with a child's mother and father. A father's stability is measured in his consistent presence, keeping his word, and stable emotional state.

4.1.a The Stress Test

Instructions: In this activity, the goal is to design and build a functioning bridge out of index cards (3x5) that can support the weight of a water bottle. The bridge must be at least one inch high x three inches wide x five inches long. You can use up to six index cards to build your bridge.

Here are two building tips:

1. Use one card for the top surface.
2. Triangles help make any structure stronger.

Process Questions:

1. Why was your bridge able or unable to support the weight of the water bottle?
2. How can you compare this exercise to our ability to handle stress or drama?
3. What are the consequences of not being able to handle stress or drama?

4.1.b What Is Stress?

4.1 Stress is the daily pressures a man experiences that can impact his function. It results from the idea there is a lack of resources to address differing intensities, frequencies, and durations of life's demands.

Not all stress is bad—sometimes stress can help us grow and develop. Next, we will look at the three common classifications of stress (CWIG, 2015; NSCDC, 2007).

Instructions: Write down three examples for each of the types of stress.

1. **Positive stress** is moderate and short-lived, causing brief increases in heart rate or mild changes in stress hormone levels. Learning to adjust to this type of stress is an important and necessary aspect of healthy development that occurs in the context of stable and supportive relationships (CWIG, NSCDC).
    a. _____
    b. _____
    c. _____
2. **Tolerable stress** is severe enough to disrupt brain architecture if unchecked, but is buffered by supportive relationships that facilitate adaptive coping and mitigate the damaging effects (CWIG, NSCDC). Tolerable stress generally occurs within a time-limited period, which gives the brain an opportunity to recover from potentially damaging effects.
    a. _____
    b. _____
    c. _____
3. **Toxic stress** is that which is severe and prolonged in the absence of the buffering protection of supportive relationships. Toxic stress disrupts brain architecture and leads to lifelong problems in learning, behavior, and both physical and mental health (CWIG, NSCDC). Relationships can mitigate the toxicity of stress.
    a. _____
    b. _____
    c. _____

4.1.c The Impact of Stress

The Child FIRST model is a way to illustrate the impact of a father's life stressors on how he functions in his role as a father. In the model, a father's role is represented by a simple machine. The father is the fulcrum and his functioning is the lever. His functioning points to his involvement, which can range from healthy to unhealthy.

Child-FIRST Model

Child-Father Involvement Resource/Stress Theoretical Model

(Williams, 2016)

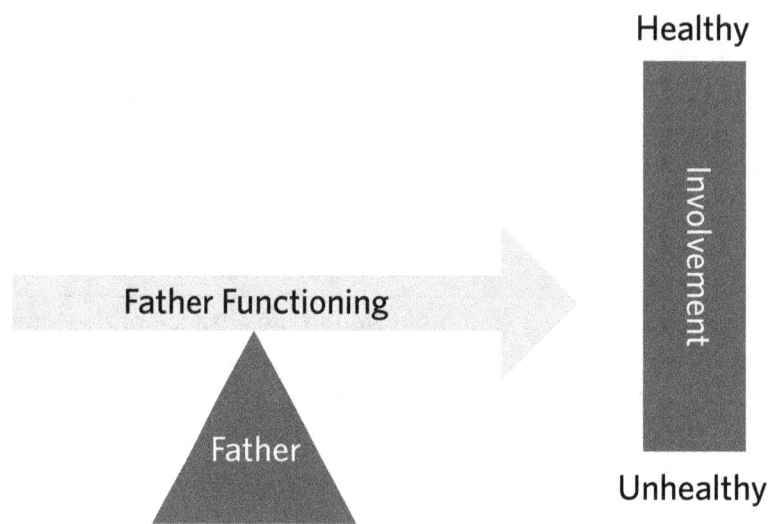

(Williams, 2016)

Process Question: How many fathers do you think are functioning with healthy involvement?

Stressors are the daily pressures a man experiences that can impact his functioning, that result from the idea there is a lack of resources to address differing intensities, frequencies, and durations of life demands.

Child-FIRST Model

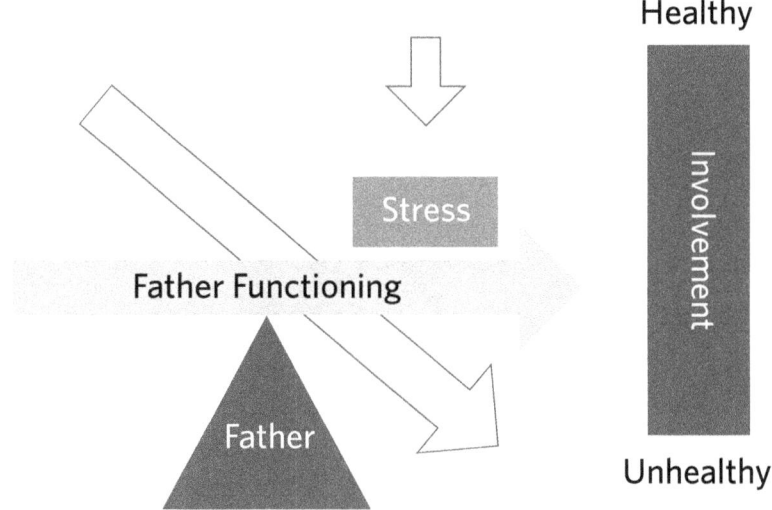

(Williams, 2016)

Process Question: What are some of the stressors that fathers face, which may interfere with his role as a father?

When fathers face life stressors or environmental risk factors, they divert their limited time, attention, and resources to address those stressors or risks and leave less time, attention, and resources to focus on the needs of the child. These stressors pile up on top of each other.

Child-FIRST Model

Process Questions: Give examples of how and why stressors can divert a father's attention to fathering.

While in many cases, stress cannot be eliminated, it can be counter balanced, with resources to address the stressors. Notice that sometimes the resources can be a positive stressor for a time, but later result in relief. One of the biggest resources is other people in stable supportive relationships.

Child-FIRST Model
Child-(Father Involvement Resource/Stress Theoretical) Model

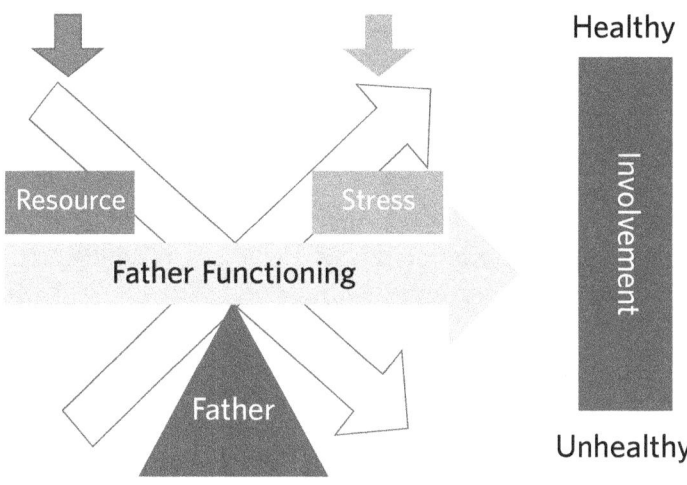

Process Questions:

1. Pair the stressors we came up with earlier with a resource that can help eliminate the stress.
2. What ways can fathers be supported to decrease stressors?
3. What ways can fathers be supported to increase resources?
4. Why don't fathers get the help they need?
5. How can we help get fathers to a place where they will seek and accept help?

The reasons for father absence are diverse and complex. Regardless of the reason for the absence or withdrawal of social capital, the question arises as to the impact of that withdrawal has on the child. Research links father absence with a host of negative social outcomes for children.

Everyone experiences stress to varying degrees and durations. However, not everyone has adequate resources to handle the stressors they face. And for these people, the perception of stressors can pile up into constant crises that hamper their functioning in life.

4.1 Stress can be a barrier to being a good father or, in the context of resources and stable support, can challenge us to develop and improve our role as a man and father.

4.2 The Trouble with Trauma

What does a child's parents' divorce have to do with his or her risk of heart disease as an adult? If a child's father had a drinking problem, is the child more likely to suffer from depression as an adult? The linking of adverse childhood experiences to later negative adult health outcomes has been said to be one of the most significant public health issues.

4.2.a Cuts Like a Knife

Trauma is defined as an inescapable horrendous experience(s) that overwhelms coping and traps a person in the body, brain, and behavior of those experiences, resulting in cutting the person off from healthy relating to self, children, and others.

Instructions: Write down the ways a physical wound is like a heart or emotional wound.

Physical Wound	Heart Wound
1	1
2	2
3	3
4	4
5	5

There are three characteristics of people who have experienced emotional trauma:

1. Reliving the heart wound
2. Avoiding things that remind you of the heart wound
3. Alarms are constantly going off for you

Process questions:

1. Do you know people who have experienced one of these characteristics?
2. What is an example of reliving the heart wound?
3. What is an example of how someone might avoid the reminders of the heart wound?
4. What is an example of someone who is constantly on edge?
5. How might these three emotional trauma characteristics affect you personally?

4.2.a The ACE Study

The ACE Study. In late 1990s, an epidemiologist, Dr. Robert Anda, and preventative medicine doctor, Dr. Vincent Felitti, led a collaborative study between the Centers for Disease Control and Prevention (CDC) and Kaiser Permanente to assess the association between childhood experiences and lifelong health (Felitti et al., 1998). An adverse childhood experience (ACE) is an extremely stressful event that can actually alter brain development and the immune system. The Adverse Childhood Experience Study (ACES) surveyed 17,337 adults for 10 types of childhood trauma and found associations between these adverse childhood experiences and later-life health and well-being outcomes (Felitti et al., 1998).

The Results. Five of the types of childhood trauma are personal, and five are household dysfunction. The findings from the ACE Study suggest that experiences of childhood trauma are major risk factors for the leading causes of illness and death, as well as poor quality of life. The majority (67%) of the largely white, middle class, college-educated respondents with good health insurance experienced trauma:

- 28 percent had been physically abused
- 27 percent experienced household substance abuse
- 23 percent had divorced parents
- 21 percent were sexually abused
- 17 percent had household members with mental illness
- 13 percent had witnessed household domestic violence
  (Felitti et al., 1998)

Adverse Childhood Experiences

Abuse	Neglect	Household Dysfunction
Physical	Physical	Mental Illness
Emotional	Emotional	Incarceration
Sexual		Mother Treated Violently
		Divorce
		Substance Abuse

Associated Outcomes

Behavior				
Lack of Physical Activity	Smoking	Alcoholism	Drug Use	Missed Work
Physical & Mental				
Severe Obesity	Diabetes	Depression	Suicide Attempts	STDs
Heart Disease	Cancer	Stroke	COPD	Broken Bones

(Centers for Disease Control and Prevention, 2016)

4.2.b The Ace Survey

This next activity will give us the experience of reviewing the ACE Survey and understanding what participants were answering to get their scores. This will also give us insight into our own childhood. **Please note you will not write down your score.**

Instructions: Read through the quiz below, and answer the questions as honestly as possible by making a mental note of an "X" in the Yes column. **For confidentiality purposes, please do not mark your actual answer in this book.**

While you were growing up, during your first 18 years of life:	Y
1. Did your parent or other adult in your household **often or very often**... Swear at you, insult you, put you down or humiliate you? **OR** act in a way that made you afraid that you might be physically hurt?	
2. Did a parent or other adult in the household **often or very often**... push, grab, slap or throw something at you? **OR** ever hit you so hard that you had marks or were injured?	
3. Did an adult or person at least five years older than you **ever**... touch or fondle you or have you touch their body in a sexual way? **OR** attempt or actually have oral, anal, or vaginal intercourse with you?	
4. Did you **often or very often** feel that... no one in your family loved you or thought you were important or special? **OR** your family didn't look out for each other, feel close to each other, or support each other?	
5. Did you **often or very often** feel that... you didn't have enough to eat, had to wear dirty clothes, and had no one to protect you? **OR** your parents were too drunk or high to take care of you, or take you to the doctor if you needed it?	
6. Was a biological parent **ever** lost to you through divorce, abandonment, or other reasons?	
7. Was your mother or stepmother **often or very often** pushed, grabbed, slapped or had something thrown at her? **OR sometimes, often, or very often** kicked, bitten, hit with a fist, or hit with something hard? **OR ever** repeatedly hit for at least a few minutes or threatened with a gun or knife?	
8. Did you live with anyone who was a problem drinker or alcoholic or who used street drugs?	
9. Was a household member depressed or mentally ill **OR** did a household member attempt suicide?	
10. Did a household member go to prison?	
Total number of Yeses	

(Felitti et al., 1998)

Instructions: Total the number of yes responses. This is your ACE score. It is for you to personally contemplate. Please do not share with others.

Process Questions

1. What was the experience of taking this quiz for you?
2. What do you think the clients experience in taking this quiz?
3. Was anybody surprised by the results?
4. What should be our response to taking this survey?

Instructions: For the next exercise, pick a number between 1 and 10 and write that number in the box below.

> "We are not a score but a score can give insight to help us overcome."
> (Williams, 2017)

The Impact of Trauma

Research that nationally estimated exposure to traumatic events found that 89.7% of those surveyed had experienced one or more traumatic events (Kilpatrick, et al., 2013). Based on the weighting of the sample, there is some ability to generalize the findings to the population of U.S. adults. This study supports that most adults have experienced some type of trauma.

The second key finding of the ACEs study is the strong relationship between the number of ACEs and later life threatening health issues. The following is a table illustrating the relationship:

1.	0 ACEs	Normal risks	All other scores compared to
2.	1 ACE	2x more likely	Alcoholic, Substance Abuser, Suicide
3.	2 ACEs	4x more likely 3x more likely 2x more likely	Alcoholic, Substance Abuser Suicide STD, Depressed
4.	3 ACEs	7x more likely 5x more likely 3x more likely 2x more likely	Attempt Suicide Alcoholic, Substance Abuser Depressed Chronic Bronchitis or Emphysema
5.	4 ACEs or more	12x more likely 7x more likely 4x more likely 3x more likely 2x more likely	Attempt Suicide Alcoholic, Substance Abuser Bronchitis or Emphysema, Depressed Heart Disease, Stroke, Cancer, Hepatitis, Poor Health, Diabetes
7.	6 ACEs or more	Live 20 years less	Earlier Death

(Felitti et al., 1998)

The experiences that happen to you as a child shape who you become as a father. All fathers were once sons. This is a reminder that many fathers may have experienced trauma where once sons. This is a reminder that many fathers may have experienced trauma as sons that have never been resolved.

Instructions: Use the following word bank and choose the right word for each statement.

Word Bank: **behavioral, mood, self-concept, attachment**

1. Fathers who were exposed to trauma as children may have experienced the uncertain and unpredictable environment that can contribute to _____ problems that result in distrust, suspicion, isolation, and relationship trouble.
2. Fathers who were exposed to trauma as children may have experienced a _____ that is unstable, and have low self-esteem, distorted body image, and strong feelings of shame and guilt.
3. Fathers who were exposed to trauma as children may have had trouble regulating their _____, as well as knowing what they want and feel and struggling to communicate it with others.
4. Fathers who were exposed to trauma as children may exhibit poor _____ control, and have self-destructive behavior, aggression, and sleep and eating disorders.

4.3 Healing, Forgiving, Making Amends, and Moving on

4.3.a Dice Activity: 2 Steps Forward, 3 Steps Back

Dice Activity: 2 Steps Forward, 3 Steps Back

Instructions: You will roll five die to match the three patterns in the order they appear. You may save the numbers you roll or re-roll as many times as you need. However, if you roll any "1" or "6" you must re-roll all the die. (Williams, 2010)

1. Four of the same number.
   example

3	3	3	3

2. Four numbers in sequence.
   example

   | 2 | 3 | 4 | 5 |

3. Two different pairs.
   example

   | 2 | 2 | 4 | 4 |

Process questions:

1. What made this activity so challenging?
2. Can you think of any way to guard against this challenge?
3. How might challenges fathers face bring them back to a place where they feel they are starting all over?

4.3.b Feel Like Giving Up?

Learned Helplessness

Seligman and Maier (1967) were doing research on classical conditioning, or the process by which an animal or human associates one thing with another. In the case of Seligman's experiment, he would ring a bell and then give a light shock to a dog. After several times, the dog reacted to the shock even before it happened: as soon as the dog heard the bell, he reacted as though he'd already been shocked.

But, then, something unexpected happened. Seligman put each dog into a large crate that was divided down the middle with a low fence. The dog could see and jump over the fence, if necessary. The floor on one side of the fence was electrified, but not on the other side. Seligman put the dog on the electrified side and administered a light shock. He expected the dog to jump to the non-shocking side of the fence.

Instead, the dogs lay down. It was as though they'd learned from the first part of the experiment that there was nothing they could do to avoid the shocks, so they gave up in the second part of the experiment. In a follow-up experiment, dogs who were not previously exposed to shocks quickly jumped the fence to escape the shocks.

Seligman described their condition as learned helplessness, or not trying to get out of a negative situation, because the past has taught you that you are helpless.

We must consider the experiences that people go through and learn how these experiences shape them and their responses. Some people have learned to be helpless and it is not easy to change. Next, we will look at how a father wound and incarceration may be traumatic barriers to fathering.

The Father Wound

In this course, we have viewed the Amos story about the wounds of an absent father and have been made aware of the number of children growing up absent their biological father. The emotional wounding or trauma an absent father may inflict on his son may cause problems in the son's future relationship with his child. There are three related experiences as a son which, together or alone, may become a challenge to a man's own role as a father. Those experiences are emotionally needing something from your father you were denied, lacking the presence of a healthy father role model, and being a victim of abuse by your father.

When you are a child, you are not likely to have the resources or capacity to resolve the wounds or trauma. Growing up to be men in American culture, we are taught to handle our own problems, so we learn to suppress our problems. Many men are uncomfortable to cry in our culture. Even though everyone says it is okay for men to cry, we don't often enough and instead learn to suppress our emotions. We are usually okay if no one brings up or talks about the issue. As a result, many men still have unresolved issues with their fathers. One of the most effective paths to healing for these men is the process of forgiveness.

Process Questions:

1. How might a father wound be a factor ~~is~~ in a man's own father absence?
2. How can you help someone identify this issue in their own life?
3. How would a person get help?
4. How might the information in this section help your work with families?
5. **Process statement:** Trauma is the unseen enemy that can sabotage the success of the father unless it is recognized and addressed.

Incarceration

In 2008, more than half (1.2 million) of the 2.3 million people who were incarcerated in U.S. prisons or jails were parents of children ages 18 and younger (The Pew Charitable Trusts, 2010). Nine out of 10 incarcerated parents were fathers of an estimated 2.7 million children who had a parent incarcerated in 2008 (The Pew Charitable Trusts). Incarcerated parents deal with separation and loss issues of their children; visitation and other contacts help them to deal with these issues and to develop and maintain their role as parents (Lincroft, 2011). Research has shown that if incarcerated fathers maintain contact with their children, they are less likely to recidivate (Lincroft). An incarcerated father's regular visits with his child are an important first step forward in the family reunification process (Lincroft).

The children also benefit from the contact by being able to process the emotional reaction of separation, to have a more realistic understanding of their father's circumstance, and be assured they are not to blame and their father will be safe (Lincroft). Research showed that when fathers are incarcerated, their children may show increases in externalizing behavior problems that are directed toward others, such as aggression, violence, or delinquency. There may also be increases in internalizing behavior problems that are directed inward, such as depression, anxiety, and difficulty paying attention (Johnson, 2009; Wakefield, 2011). Another study reported a strong association between paternal incarceration and increases in mental and physical problems in young adults, including depression, PTSD, anxiety, high cholesterol, asthma, and overall health problems (Lee, Fang, & Luo, 2013).

Process Questions

1. Why is it important to stay in contact with your child even when incarcerated?
2. What are things you can do to stay in contact?
3. How can a father improve his situation while incarcerated?

4.3.c Forgiveness and Moving Forward

Fathering History Survey

Instructions: Evaluate each statement by marking a number that reflects your response where 5 means strongly agree and 1 means strongly disagree. Follow the instructions to determine your total score and what your score suggests.

Group 1					
1. My father was supportive of me.	1	2	3	4	5
2. It was easy to get close to my father.	1	2	3	4	5
3. As a child, I knew what my father felt about me.	1	2	3	4	5
4. My father regularly showed his affection for me.	1	2	3	4	5
5. My father was a good example	1	2	3	4	5
Total					
Group 2					
1. My father used alcohol or drugs often.	1	2	3	4	5
2. My father was mostly absent during my childhood.	1	2	3	4	5
3. My father abused me or another family member.	1	2	3	4	5
4. My father was sexually unfaithful to my mother.	1	2	3	4	5
5. My father was convicted of a crime or committed illegal acts.	1	2	3	4	5
Total					
Group 3					
1. I read parenting literature often.	1	2	3	4	5
2. I have a close friend who supports me.	1	2	3	4	5
3. I am regularly involved in a small group.	1	2	3	4	5
4. I keep in contact with my kids frequently.	1	2	3	4	5
5. I am seeking ways to improve/strengthen my parenting.	1	2	3	4	5
Total					

(Williams, 2010)

(Group 1 Total) _____ subtracted from
(Group 2 Total) _____

Sub-Total _____ added to

(Group 3 Total) _____

Total Score _____

Results Range −15 to +45

Strong Heritage	34–45
Solid Foundation	33–19
Challenged Position	18–7
Wounded Heart	−15–6

Process Questions

1. How might your own history with your father or the father of your children influence your attitudes and behaviors towards other fathers?
2. What are ways you can prevent this from happening?

Instructions: In the first column, write down what forgiveness is not. In the second column, write down what forgiveness is.

What forgiveness is not:	What forgiveness is:

Forgiveness is a process and choice you have the power to make. You can grant forgiveness to someone who may not deserve it, or ask for it and free yourself from the offense. This can start you on the road to healing.

Forgiveness Letter

Instructions: Write down a forgiveness letter

1. Name the wound
2. Write down your worst pain
3. Share it with someone
4. Destroy the letter

4.4 The Dad Plan

Fathering Skill: Become a better dad by healing from my past through forgiveness and lowering stress and moving forward.

Remember to use SMART goals for your plan to turn your life around.

Instructions: Answer the following questions to create your dad plan to become a better dad.

1. What is my specific SMART (Specific, Measurable, Achievable, Realistic, Timetable) goal for growing in cultural awareness?
2. What can I do every day this week to grow more culturally aware?
3. When and where will I do this?
4. Who will hold me accountable?

5.0 Becoming Dad

GOAL

To become a better dad
I will be humble and seek to learn
Ways to improve as a parent, co-parent and citizen
And let this passion to be better burn.

OBJECTIVES

1. Better relational skills
2. Better co-parenting skills
3. Better fathering skills

To be the best dad we can be, we need to stand up against myths that will get in the way of our growth and development as a father. One myth is that we are an island and can do it all alone. No man is an island; we were created for relationships and in the context of relationships we grow and develop. We need others and others need us.

Another myth is that we know all we need to know about being a father. There are no perfect fathers; we all have room to learn. Although Becoming Dads is a solid program, it is just scratching the surface of all that is available to learn on this lifelong journey of fatherhood. The best way to take advantage of all that is to be humble and open to learning from others in their successes and failures, from the young and old, strangers and family, and the list goes on. We even learn from our own children. Are you ready to be better?

5.1 Better Relational Skills

5.1.a The Family Tree

A genogram is a graphical representation of a person's family relationships. In this exercise, we will develop a simple genogram to write about the parents you spent the most time with as a child.

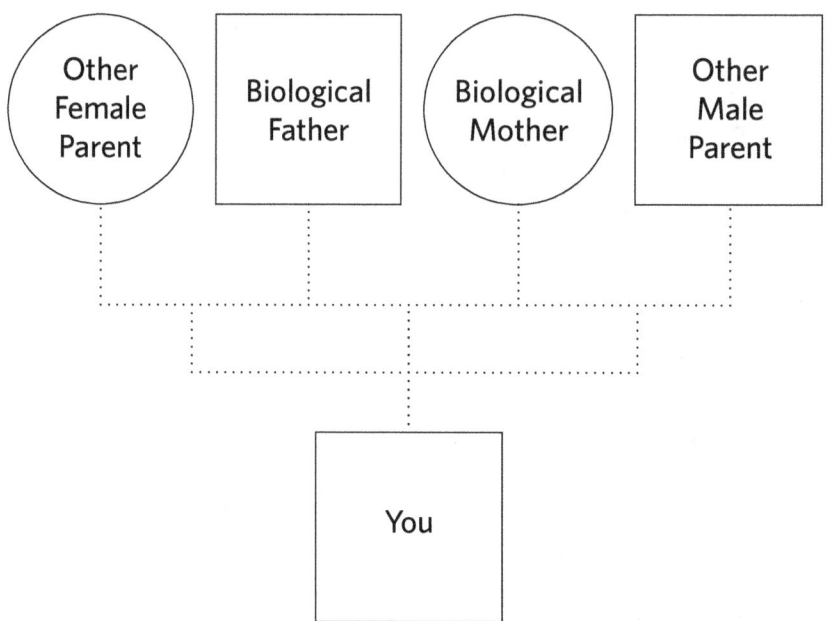

Instructions: Complete the following actions:

1. If you know them, write the name of your biological father and mother above their box.
2. Draw over the dotted lines to connect the two parents you spent the most time living with to each other (whether with both biological parents or one biological parent and their partner).
3. If one of your "parents" was a partner of your biological parent, write that name above the shape.
4. Draw over dotted lines to connect the two parents to you.

Process Questions:

1. Were your "parents" married; if not, did it matter to you?
2. Describe what your relationship was like with your father and/or your other male parent.
3. Describe your relationship with your mother or your other female parent.
4. How did your parent's relationship or parent's partnering relationships impact you?
5. Describe the things you liked about your family.
6. Describe the things you did not like about your family.
7. What would you change for your family?

5.1.b Family Needs

Be Known

Using a cognitive and behavior perspective to Maslow's hierarchy of needs, Ryan and Deci argue that there are three basic or core innate psychological needs, described as competence, relatedness, and autonomy. From the study of this theory, Dr. Henriques suggests you can go further by identifying the need an individual has to be known and valued by himself/herself and important to others.

Being "known" means the individual is able to share his or her full experiences, private thoughts, and public image with important others. It can be considered the single most important variable in human development in terms of outcomes regarding character structure and well-being.

Instructions: What do you know about your child? Following are some questions we need to ask our child regularly, because the answers often change. Write your answer to the question in the space provided. As a take-home assignment, find out your child's answers to the questions to see how many you get right.

Awareness Quiz

1. What is your child's favorite color?

Your answer	Your child's answer

2. Who is your child's best friend?

Your answer	Your child's answer

3. What is your child's favorite game?

Your answer	Your child's answer

4. What is your child's favorite movie or TV show?

Your answer	Your child's answer

5. What is your child's favorite food, drink, dessert, and candy?

Your answer	Your child's answer

6. What is your child's favorite song?

Your answer	Your child's answer

7. What is your child's favorite book?

Your answer	Your child's answer

8. What does your child want to be when he or she grows up?

Your answer	Your child's answer

Your child's wants to be known by you, so study your child.

Belong

Another core family need is the need we possess to belong. Attachment theory explores the deep and enduring emotional bond that connects one person to another across time and space (Bowlby, 1969).

We are born love and care-dependent, and throughout life have a need for important others. The "others" refers to those people the individual cares about and usually includes: 1) family of origin, 2) present family, 3) romantic partners/interests, 4) close friends, 5) peers, and 6) social identities/group affiliations.

> **Process Question**: How can you show your children that they have a place they belong with you, especially if you do not live in their home?

Be Fulfilled

Being valued in a family means that one is prized, admired, and/or loved, and that one's interests are respected and honored. It naturally follows that family members would be provided care and the meeting of their needs.

In the McMaster's model of family functioning, Epstein, Bishop, and Baldwin (1984), share that the model's stated assumptions about the primary function of the family is to provide a setting for the development and maintenance of family members on a biological, social, and psychological level. The functioning of the family is grouped into three areas: basic tasks, developmental tasks, and crisis tasks.

Being filled is having all the three tasks of the family fulfilled. The basic tasks include the family member being provided items such as food, clothing, money, transportation and housing. The developmental tasks include fostering healthy growth through all the developmental life cycle. The hazardous tasks include handling crises within the family due to internal or external factors.

> **Fatherhood is about providing for the needs of our child physically, emotionally, socially, and spiritually.**

5.1.c Speaking

Instructions: Review the sayings on speaking and words and determine if they hold true today.

1. "Sticks and stones may break my bones, but words will never harm me."
2. "Be slow to speak and quick to listen."
3. "No words can help you more or hurt you more than the words spoken by your biological parents."
4. "Children should be seen, but not heard."
5. "The power of life and death is in the tongue."
6. "Loose lips sink ships."
7. "Out of the abundance of the heart the mouth speaks."

Instructions: Read the following statements and determine which word from the word bank best fits in the blank.

1. **think**	4. **build**	6. **body**
2. **known**	5. **blaming and**	**language**
3. **know**	**criticizing**	7. **open-ended**

1. It is important that you _____ about what you want before you speak.
2. A goal of speaking is to be _____, who you are, and what you want and need.
3. Another goal of speaking is to _____ others, who they are, and what they want and need.
4. Another important reason we speak is to b_____ others up and not tear them down.
5. We should avoid _____ and _____ others.
6. Make sure what you say aligns with your _____.
7. _____ questions encourage a full, meaningful answer from your child's own thoughts and feelings that help you know them better.

Process Questions:

1. Did your parents speak to you in demeaning ways?
2. Did people speak things into your life that built you up?
3. What words have been spoken to you in the past that still affect you today?
4. What's wrong with this statement, "I just don't understand my child; he doesn't listen to me."?

5.1.d Listening

"Listening to someone's thoughts and feelings affirms their self-worth." —grw

When you LISTEN, you must be quiet first; then you should say what you hear the other person saying. The goal of listening is to understand the other person.

Instructions: Communication can be divided into three components that comprise it. Write in what percent of communication are words, sounds and body language.

Words	Sounds	Body Language	Total
%	%	%	100%

Process Question: What does this tell you about communication?

Instructions: Take 30 seconds and fill in the blanks for the different aspects of listening in the Chinese word *ting* from the following list: Heart, Attention, Eyes, Body, Mind, and Ears.

1. _____
2. _____
3. _____
4. _____
5. _____
6. _____

Ting (traditional Chinese word for "listen")

1. To hear (twice as much as you speak)
2. To think (being in the moment)
3. To be present (be there)
4. To see (face to face)
5. To focus (not distracted by other things)
6. To feel (empathy)

Reflective listening involves paying respectful attention to the content and feelings of your child, to let them know that they were heard and understood by sharing it back.

The reflecting skills involve the following:

1. Non-verbal gestures and brief one or two word statements that you are listening
2. Reflecting the content of the essence of what was said in your own words
3. Reflecting the feelings to the others in your own words

Instructions: In the first scenario, the facilitator will play the role of the child, who does the talking, and the father, who uses reflective listening in the first scenario. In the second scenario, you will pair up and take turns being the father and child, so you can practice reflective listening.

1. Child: "You always fight with mom. Why can't you get along with her? When you both raise your voices and yell at each other and say bad things, I get scared something bad is going to happen. I love you both. I wish you would stop."

2. Child: "You promised you were coming to pick me up yesterday and you didn't. I was waiting and waiting for you and you never came. I cried all afternoon. Mommy said, something must have come up. But why didn't you even call? I don't believe you anymore. You can't even do what you say you are going to do."

Process Question: How do you think reflective listening can be helpful in your relationship with your child and others?

5.2 Co-Parenting

Co-parenting requires the parents to work together while actively making individual contributions for the benefit of the children. Co-parenting in a family is critical to the success of the children and family, even when the parents do not live together.

5.2.a Family Sculpturing

Instructions: We are going to do a family sculpture using three chairs. Volunteers will have an opportunity to arrange the chairs in a way to represent a healthy family. They will arrange the chairs, identify which chair represents the father, mother, and child, and then say how the arrangement highlights a healthy family.

5.2.b Getting Past the Drama

What do you work towards when you have a family? You should COOPERATE, meaning that you both try to find an answer or solution that works for both of you. These are the steps for cooperating:

1. Take turns talking and listening
2. Offer trades
3. Stop and calm down if you are angry

Problem Solving

After you have scheduled a time for everyone involved to get together and work on solving the problem, it is a good idea to make a plan. The following steps can help make the process easier:

1. State the problem.
2. Write or discuss the results you want. Be sure to be as specific as possible.
3. List all possible solutions.
   Listen to everyone's ideas, and do not dismiss anyone's idea as stupid or impossible.
4. Review the list together.
   Go over the list with everyone needed to solve the problem.
5. Each person should choose two solutions he is willing to carry out.
6. Decide on a solution.
7. After your group has decided on a solution, decide what tasks need to be done and who will carry them out. Plan to meet to evaluate the progress of the solution.

5.2.c Co-parenting Tips

1. Respect her and practice treating her like you want to be treated.
2. Practice trying to see things from your child and your child's mother's point of view.
3. Communicate directly and never through the children.
4. Share information with your partner.
5. Support your co-parent's role with your child and to your child.
6. Recognize the boundary of her home. Be careful with advice and don't criticize.
7. Refresh and work on yourself when you don't have your child(ren).

Instructions: From this section, describe what you can work on to improve your co-parenting, whether or not you live with your child's mother.

_____

_____

_____

_____

5.3 Better Dads Skills

5.3.a Investing Your Time

What does a healthy father look like? There are three important aspects of fathering skills:

1. The father (and mother) is in charge of the family.
2. The father gives everyone room (including himself) to be close and apart.
3. The father is flexible when it comes to change.

The two important roles of the father are to lead and model. To be successful in life, children need to learn to feel good about themselves and to get along with other people. The father needs to commit to help the child develop a positive sense of himself/herself and develop the ability to make and keep friends. One of the ways that the father acts as a leader is by making rules for the family.

5.3.b Leading and Role Modeling

Rules without relationship leads to rebellion. Here are three guidelines for making rules:

1. Make rules for what you want, not don't want.
2. Make rules with results you can see or measure.
3. State the rule in a sentence and be specific.

You and your families have been through many changes. Changes occur as people get older, move into their own apartments, get married, get new jobs, have children, and die. Change can be exciting, but it can also be difficult. The following are some general rules for change:

1. **Expect change.** Remember that changes are normal. All families go through change—some ordinary and some not so ordinary.
2. **Stress is a signal that change is necessary.**
   Do you know how to tell when you are feeling stress? It could be that you feel worried or upset, or you could be angry or sick. When you are feeling like this, it probably means that you need to make a change in some area of your life; maybe find a new way of doing something.

3. **Expect to feel resistance in others and yourself.** Change is hard. People usually try to continue without making any changes for as long as possible. Just remember that change is normal, and it is also normal to not want to change. Hopefully, this will help reduce the amount of time you spend fighting change.
4. **Take one step at a time.** Change takes time. It easier to deal with if you are able to focus on one small step at a time.
5. **Ask someone for help if you are stuck.**
   Family, friends, teachers, and religious leader are all good sources of help.
6. **Anticipate areas where children will need a rule and make it.** When the guests arrive, the television is to be turned off.
7. **Get your children's thoughts on rules that affect them, especially as they get older.** Then, you make the final decision. "You want to drive the car to a dance and we're worried about your showing off or getting in an accident."
8. **"Tell us why you think you are ready for it."**
9. **Only make rules you are prepared to enforce.**
10. **Consider your own comfort**, as well as your child's needs, in deciding on rules. For example, "You would like to stay up until 10 p.m., but your mother and I need some time to ourselves. Bedtime is 9 p.m."
11. **Expect resistance.** Feel free to change any rule you made which no longer gets the result you want. For example, "Now that summer is here, it's okay to get home by 6 p.m. instead of 4 p.m."

Family Meeting

A good way for families to solve problems and to know what is going on with each other is to have a family meeting. The following things should happen in a family meeting:

- Have one meeting per week.
- The meeting should last no more than one hour.
- Only one person should speak at a time.
- Making fun of each other and name-calling cannot happen.
- Everyone will have a turn to speak.
- Everyone should say one thing that is going right.
- Any problems should be identified.
- Pick one problem to solve.
- Stay focused on what people want and how to get it, not on complaints
- Plan a fun activity for next week.

Our group can also have "family meetings" to help us make decisions, plan activities, and solve problems. In our first meeting, we will work together to decide what kind of rules we want to make for participation in our group. Let's try to make rules for what we want, not for what we don't want. We also need to decide on consequences, both good and bad.

5.3.c Caring for Your Child

Instructions: Find the words below that describe nurturing.

Nurture Word Find

A	F	N	S	H	R	E	T	A	M	L	Y
O	C	I	U	S	R	T	S	N	O	A	H
K	G	M	S	T	E	E	I	A	L	C	P
P	A	U	A	T	V	A	F	P	R	T	I
M	L	D	H	O	B	E	N	U	V	C	H
Z	A	E	L	N	E	U	H	H	Q	E	S
E	R	K	F	S	B	C	M	S	B	L	D
P	U	X	E	I	S	T	D	P	U	A	N
J	T	B	L	U	R	S	F	P	L	U	I
R	O	W	J	L	P	N	I	Y	A	G	E
A	N	K	D	F	H	O	N	K	B	H	R
V	O	T	E	R	A	C	N	A	N	I	F

Word Bank: Hug, Kiss, Fist Bump, Make up, Love, Care, Joke, Laugh, Play.

Be affectionate especially as they get older. Kids need love, but not just words alone.

Kids do understand a loving touch. Hugging them, snuggling them, and kissing them makes them feel loved. It's a basic way humans communicate love, but some fathers feel awkward showing love in this way. However, we need to get over it. A kid needs to feel loved, always, and you have within your power a guaranteed way to make them know they're loved. A kid who knows he or she is loved is a happy kid—the kind of kid that runs and jumps into your arms when they see you.

You will never, never regret being affectionate with your children, because you will be able to send a "you're loved" message right to your children's heart anytime with just a simple peck on the forehead, a quick hug before school, or even just tousling their hair as they walk by. A dad's loving touch is amazingly powerful; it sends a message to your child that words can't always convey. (By the way, high-fiving doesn't count. A high-five is a celebration, not a sign of affection.)

Treat your kid the way you wanted to be treated when you were a kid. Take a look back on how you were raised. Look back at how your dad showed, or didn't show, his love for you—how he disciplined you, encouraged you, criticized you, and molded you. If you had a great dad, now's your chance to take everything he showed you and put it to good use.

If you didn't have a great dad, this is your chance, your golden opportunity, to make up for every fatherly injustice he did to you by being to your child a much more sensitive, involved, loving dad than he was to you. This is your chance to show your dad, and the world, "This is what being a good dad looks like." Provide your child with a level of love, patience, understanding, and affection that shows your own dad how it's done.

Don't ever abuse your kid. Ever. The same goes for your wife. There is never, ever a reason to hit a woman or abuse a child. It is the height of cowardice and a disgrace to fathers everywhere to hurt any woman or child. It is impossible to be a great dad if you hurt your child or your child's mommy, even once. It dishonors you, your entire life, and everything you've worked this hard to achieve. Pass this on to your kids.

Besides hitting, never be verbally cruel to your child. Never call him stupid, an idiot, or any name that makes him think he's less than the special child he is. Make it your goal to give your kid so much love and praise that it gives him a high self-esteem problem.

5.4 The Dad Plan

Fathering Skill: Become a better dad by improving my relational skills, my co-parenting and my role as a father.

Remember to use SMART goals for your plan to turn your life around.

Instructions: Answer the following questions to create your dad plan to become a better dad.

1. What is my specific SMART (Specific, Measurable, Achievable, Realistic, Timetable) goal for growing in cultural awareness?
2. What can I do every day this week to grow more culturally aware?
3. When and where will I do this?
4. Who will hold me accountable?

6.0 Moving Forward

GOAL

To become a better dad
No matter how tough I won't quit or give up
Through the support of my faith, family and community
Until my last breath and my eyes finally shut.

OBJECTIVES

1. Child support
2. Employment
3. Overcoming addiction

6.1 Child support

6.1.a Activity: Aircraft Carrier Support

Instructions: The facilitator will instruct the class on making a Dart paper airplane. Once the Dart has been constructed, you will have an opportunity for a couple of practice flights.

The Dart is a "jet" and a designated table will be an "aircraft carrier." The objective is throwing your Dart in such a way as to land it on the table. Once all Darts have been completed, we will take turns to attempt to land the plane on an aircraft carrier (table).

Process Questions

1. How does an aircraft carrier support the aircraft?
2. What is child support?
3. How much support should you give your child?
4. What are other ways you support your child?
5. Can you think of a situation where you would not support your child?

Child support is intended to be a minimum amount paid by the noncustodial parent to contribute to the financial needs of the child.

6.1.b How DADS Can Help

There is no worse description of single fathers who have gone underground than the label "deadbeat dad." This is terribly unjust condemnation to put upon a man who finds himself in the no-win situation of being damned if he does (seeking legitimate work and paying what the system says he owes for child support) and damned if he doesn't (going off the radar, doing "under the table" day labor jobs, or engaging in criminal behavior). It is not as simple as it may sound; the situations are more often complex.

Instruction: List three factors that get in the way of men paying child support.

1. _____
2. _____
3. _____

Process Question: How can we get past these barriers?

Next, we will review the five steps to *Becoming Dads*—dads who are striving to be better:

1. **Face the Reality**—The first step is an honest look at our current situation of housing, transportation, legal issues, addiction, family violence, income, employment ,and how you all can be more involved with your child(ren).
2. **Turn Around**—The second step is making a decision to change your situation—to repent or stop going the way you've been going and going another way. Be willing

to take the time and make the effort to make the changes to become the dad your child needs.
3. **My Dad Plan**—Make a plan to become a safe person for your child: recovering from addiction and family violence, giving your child a place to stay in a home, transportation to get where he or she needs to go, a father who is not in danger of incarceration, a father who can provide for the needs of his child, and a father who has time for his child.
4. **The Parenting Plan**—A parenting plan or custody plan outlines how you and the other parent will continue to care and provide for your children after you separate. An effective plan contains a parenting time schedule that shows when your child is with each parent and how the exchange is made, who has legal custody and the authority to make decisions about the child, medical and health care information that explains how the parent pays for medical and dental cost and who provides medical insurance, where your child will attend school and who pays and engages at the school, what are the guidelines to follow in raising your child, and how the parents will communicate and work together.
5. **Work with DADS**—Divine Alternatives for Dads Services is here to come alongside of you. We will help you understand and work with the system, show how faith can help you turn your situation around, help you take practical steps to improve your situation, and be your fans who will believe in you and encourage you with hope that life can be different for you and your child.

6.1 The majority of men want to support their child and DADS can help you support your child.

6.1.c Frequently Asked Questions

Child support is a topic that tends to polarize all parties involved. Though in some situations mothers pay child support to custodial fathers, in the vast majority of cases mothers are the custodial parents and non-custodial fathers pay child support. So, how does the child support system work, and what does a father need to know in order to manage his obligations?

The State Program for Parents

DADS was the model for the Alternative Solutions Program, a statewide initiative within the Division of Child Support (DCS) aimed at helping parents toward self-sufficiency. DCS puts great value on the noncustodial parent's role in their communities and with their families. While most parents pay their child support, others have trouble meeting their responsibility. Their well-rounded approach to child support services works as a bridge between community groups and the people they help, dealing with issues, such as joblessness, housing, medical and legal issues, and transition from jail and prison.

The Alternative Solutions Program links parents with government and community groups to increase their ability to get a job and be financially stable. When you take part in the Alternative Solutions Program, your case worker will work with you to create an action plan for you that could:

- work with local partners that can help with finding a job, training, housing, food, medical and legal resources
- help lower your monthly DCS payments or state-owed debt
- help with license suspension and other case actions

With a database of over 3,500 community resources in the state, we can connect you to the services you need.

How Long Child Support Lasts

Generally, the law requires a person paying child support to make those payments until (1) your child is no longer a minor, unless the child has special needs; (2) the child becomes active-duty military, (3) your parental rights are terminated through adoption or another legal process, or (4) your minor child is declared "emancipated" by a court—that is, declared an adult earlier than normal because of the ability to be self-supporting.

How a Custody Decision Impacts Child Support

Both parents have a responsibility to support their children financially. When a divorce occurs and one parent has physical custody of the children, that parent's responsibility is fulfilled by being the custodial parent. The other parent then makes a child support payment, which fulfills that non-custodial parent's financial responsibilities. In the case of joint custody, the amount of child support each pays is normally calculated by the court, considering the percentage each parent contributes to the couple's joint income and the percentage of time each parent has physical custody of the children.

Child Support Responsibilities When Not Married

The obligation to support a child is not conditioned by marriage. If you are a parent, you have a responsibility to financially support your offspring. Your parental responsibilities can be legally determined either through your acknowledgment that you are a parent, by the fact that you had welcomed the child into your home as your own, or as established by a paternity test.

State laws vary somewhat on the definition of a parent, so if there is some doubt about your parentage, you will want to consult with a family law attorney in your state.

It also happens at times that a man who fathered a child may not be asked to pay child support until the child's mother receives public assistance. In that case, the government may come to the father seeking back child support to reimburse the government for their assistance payments. Many fathers have been "blindsided" by these orders many years after the fact.

Stepfather's Financial Liability

A stepfather is not financially liable. However, if he legally adopts the children, and thus terminates the parental rights of the biological father, the stepfather becomes liable for their financial support.

How the Amount of Child Support Is Determined

Each state in the United States is required by federal law to establish guidelines that are used to calculate child support due from parents based largely on their income and expenses. Because states have a fair amount of discretion in setting these guidelines, child support payments required vary widely between states, even under the same circumstances. But, normally, the courts will take into account issues like the standard of living of the child prior to the divorce, the specific needs of the child, the resources of the custodial parent, and the non-custodial parent's ability to pay. Because in most states judges are allowed wide discretion in setting these payments, it is important for a non-custodial father to get as much information on the table with the court up front, to make the payments are fair as possible.

How Earnings Change Impacts Calculations If Underemployed or Returning to School

This depends on the judge and the circumstances. But, generally, a child support payment would not be reduced if a father quit a full-time job and returned to school. If he became unemployed and then took a lower paying job, a reconsideration of the amount of child support due might be appropriate.

Consequences of Not Making Child Support Payments as Ordered

Not staying current on your child support obligations is called "big trouble." You are inviting a lot of legal involvement in your life and finances if you don't live up to your mandated child support obligations. Additionally, it can hurt your credibility with the court and with state enforcement officials if you want to later make changes to your parenting plan, your custody arrangements or other aspects of the legal relationship with your kids and your former spouse.

The court order entered as a part of your divorce and custody process defines the amount and payment schedule, as well as other conditions that might lead to recalibrating your commitments. These conditions might prescribe how much of a new raise might be added to your support obligations, or what you can do with a windfall like an inheritance or an insurance settlement.

Failing to meet the schedule is seen as defying an order of the court and could land you in jail, resulting in a garnishment of your wages, intercepting your tax refund, seizing property, suspending your business license or driver's license, or other serious consequences.

Garnishment is sometimes the most difficult, as it involves your employer holding back some, most, or all of your income and remitting it to the state. When paying your back obligations involves your employer, it could create some unintended negative consequences at work.

While Title III of the federal Consumer Credit Protection Act prohibits an employer from firing an employee for having a garnishment for any single indebtedness, you could be in trouble with your employer for multiple garnishments. Others that could come beyond your child support garnishments (like back taxes or other debts) could result in your being fired. So, this is clearly something you want to avoid at almost any cost.

If you are having difficulty meeting your child support obligations, you might consider creating a more realistic budget, reducing your expenses, finding less expensive housing, getting a cheaper car, or negotiating with creditors to lower your monthly debt obligation payments. These may seem like drastic measures, and may really change your life, but a more austere lifestyle may be in order so you can meet your obligations and provide for the care of your children.

If you become unemployed, take a pay cut, have large medical bills, or have some other extenuating circumstance, it is important that you begin the process immediately to have your child support amount modified.

You would start by contacting your state's child support enforcement office and requesting to file a formal motion to modify your child support obligations. It is in your best interest to start this process as soon as something significant changes. In most cases, the law prohibits a judge from retroactively reducing a child support payment, even if a reduction is reasonable after the fact. You will remain on the hook for the amounts required before the effective date of the modified child support order.

Getting behind on your child support payments is something you need to think seriously about. Neglecting this important responsibility can have far-reaching consequences and is a lot more critical than many other choices you can make when times get tough financially. Just go in with your eyes wide open.

Options If Your Children's Mother Refuses to Pay Court-Ordered Support

Federal law requires the state or district attorney to help you collect delinquent child support payments. Most states have an entire bureaucracy—usually called something like the Office of Recovery Services—available to collect these payments, and you should start there.

If Your Circumstances Have Changed

Only the court can change a mandated child support payment, so any modification would have to be submitted to a judge. If both spouses agree on a change, it is usually a pretty simple process. When you don't agree, the request will be submitted by your family law attorney for a hearing. The spouse who wants to make a change over the other's objection has the burden to show what has changed and why a different amount (higher or lower) should be required. Temporary changes might be the result of a medical emergency, a change in employment status, or a short-term economic hardship on the part of the receiving parent.

A permanent change in child support is often considered when income changes due to a remarriage, either parent has a job change that affects ability to pay, or the child involved has new and different needs than were contemplated when the original amount was set.

Withholding Child Support If Your Ex Doesn't Honor Custody or Visitation Orders

This is one of the biggest complaints of non-custodial fathers. Unfortunately, you cannot do this. Child support payments and visitation are considered by the law to be totally separate issues. If your ex is not living up to the custody decree by providing visitation as required, you will need to go back to court to enforce the court order. You have an obligation to financially support your children, regardless of any visitation issues.

6.2 Employment

Employment is a necessity to meet our needs and the needs of our child. There are many paths to employment which include education, special training, starting your own business, or working for someone else. In this section, we will explore important conditions for finding desirable employment.

6.2.a Activity: 30-Second Commercial

A "30-second commercial" (3SC) could be your best chance to make a good impression on a potential employer. And, just like a television advertiser who is trying to sell a product will spend time and money getting it just right, you can spend time and practice to get it just right, so you can be hired.

What does a 3SC contain? Here is an outline of the 3SC:

1. **Greeting**: (pleasant smile, firm handshake, speak clearly) "I am pleased to meet you; my name is (your first and last name)."
2. **Education, Experience & Skills**: (where did you go to school, what did you study, who did you work for, what did you do, any special skills)
3. **Strengths**: (character qualities such as: hard working, creative, diligent, etc.)
4. **Accomplishments**: (recognition or accomplishments that highlight your strengths)
5. **Goal**: (what work or career are you looking for)

Instructions: Make a list of items for each category and then use these items to create your 30-second commercial.

Greeting	1.
Education, Experience, and Skills	1. 2. 3.
Strengths	1. 2. 3.
Accomplish-ments	1. 2. 3.
Goal	1.

6.2.b Soft Skills

Instructions: In the diagram below, label the outline of the man with your top five characteristics of being a team player (having important soft skills).

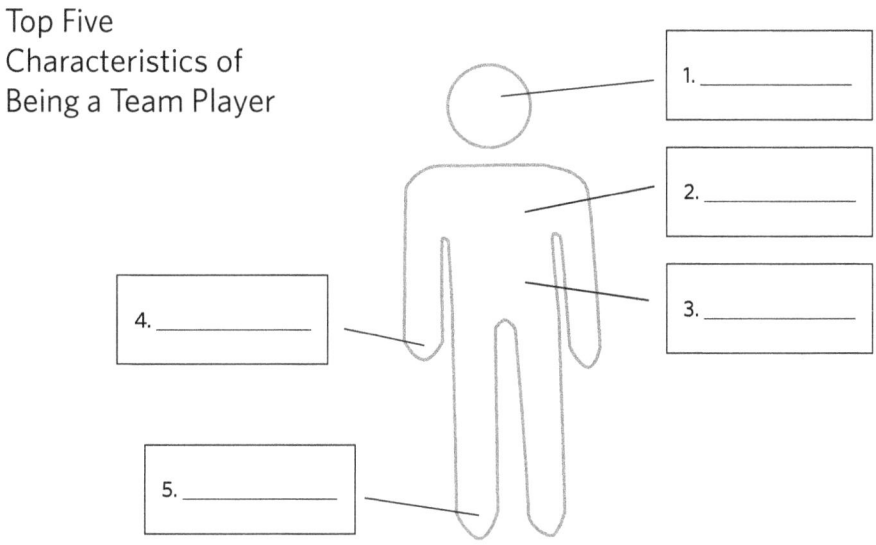

Top Five Characteristics of Being a Team Player

1. _____
2. _____
3. _____
4. _____
5. _____

A Positive Attitude

Employers seek employees who take the initiative and have the motivation to get the job done in a reasonable period of time. A positive attitude gets the work done and motivates others to do the same without dwelling on the challenges that inevitably come up in any job.

It is the enthusiastic employee who creates an environment of goodwill and who provides a positive role model for others. A positive attitude is something that is most valued by supervisors and co-workers, and makes the job more pleasant and fun to go to each day.

A Good Work Ethic

A strong work ethic is something a potential employer will want to see. It can be demonstrated by your ability to follow through on your duties and responsibilities and always ensure the work is done completely and according to procedures. Commitment is another characteristic that goes along with a strong work ethic. Be at work on time, do what you were hired to do, meet targets and deadlines, and work to the best of your ability. What more could an employer ask?

Excellent Communication Skills

This includes the ability to communicate clearly and effectively in many mediums: by email, verbally, with lists and phone messages, on the phone, and with body language. Communication also includes listening skills and the ability to follow directions and provide feedback.

Problem Solving

Companies are looking for people who are motivated to take on challenges with minimal direction. Employees should see when something needs to be done and react accordingly.

A Team Player

Employers and managers like to have people working with them and for them who can get along with their colleagues and who can work with others effectively in different circumstances.

Leadership

Do you see this individual being a significant part of your company and leading future employees of the firm? Leadership begins with self-confidence, and is molded by positive reinforcement and repetitive success.

Innovative Thinking

Companies always need creative team members to help find new solutions. One of the benefits of new hires is new ideas, but to make sure you get new ideas you need creative thinkers.

6.2.c Preparing for Employment

Picking it up: When you pick up or drop off an application, be prepared for an interview. You never know if they will have a few minutes and are in a hurry to hire someone. Also, dress appropriately, because even though you may not get an interview that day, the secretary or person who takes the application may be asked by the interviewer what they thought of you. First impressions are important; you only get one time to make them.

Read carefully: Read the entire form carefully. Know what is being asked before filling out the form. Employers may use the application form to judge how well you follow instructions and how careful you may be as an employee. Fill in the blanks, and answer all questions. Answer completely, accurately, and truthfully. When something doesn't apply to you, write N/A for "not-applicable." Check your answers for correct spelling, grammar, punctuation, completeness, and accuracy.

Ink/Type: Use blue or black ink or type the application. Print clearly. No funky colors.

Salary expected: Employers may use this question to screen out applicants. It is best to give a salary range or to respond with "negotiable." Use one of these responses even if you know the wage. This leaves you room to negotiate a higher wage.

Personal information: If you don't have a phone, give a number where messages can be left for you.

Education and training: List academic, vocational, and professional education and schools attended. Be prepared to attach copies of certificates or other documents. If you are planning to attend college, write "Plan to attend XYZ College" and when.

Work experience: Always list the most recent employer first. Give complete and accurate names, dates, addresses, phone numbers, job titles, dates of employment, etc. Use your resume as a guide. Make sure the information presented in the application agrees with the information in your resume. Explain gaps in your work history.

Special job-related skills: Use action verbs to list your special job-related skills, training, licenses, and accomplishments. List the types of equipment/tools that you can use. This will make you stand out from other applicants. The job description can provide clues about important skills.

Reason for leaving: Be careful when giving your reason for leaving a previous job. Even if your previous boss was a jerk, you should never be negative. Acceptable answers include: "school conflict," "conflicting hours," "better opportunities for advancement," "lack of work," and "seasonal employment."

References: Most employers will call references, but they also may request a written evaluation by mail. Many employers can only tell dates worked and if they would re-hire you. Therefore, you may want to use teachers, counselors, principals, coaches, ministers, etc. as references. (Do not use relatives.) Be sure to ask for their permission and verify where they can be reached. Provide complete and accurate information about three (or more) people who can speak highly of you.

Last details: Sign (don't print) your name and include the current date. Check carefully that you have completed the application. Once you fill out an application, it is a binding document; any misinformation could be grounds for termination. If you are asked when you can begin work, be sure to allow enough time to give at least two weeks' notice to your current employer.

Instructions: Fill out the application.

Personal Information
Name, Address, Phone

Position Applying For

Desired Wage

Have you ever been convicted of a felony?

Employment History (Last three jobs)

Education

Special Skills

References

6.2 We need employment that provides a livable wage to meet all our personal obligations, including meeting the needs of our children.

6.3 Addictions

Addiction is like a tornado; it is often not seen coming until it is too late. It tears through your life and the lives of people you know. In its wake, it leaves of path of destruction for everything it touches. Once caught in the addiction tornado, your life can spin in a cycle of drugs, crime, and incarceration. Addiction is a matter of life and death.

However, there is hope, and many people have found a path to recovery. In this section, we seek to better understand addiction and how we can get on the path to recover.

6.3 Activity: Paper Football Game

Instructions: The facilitator will instruct you on making a simple football and explaining the rules. We will pair up and play a four-minute game of paper football.

1. Move the ball by flicking with thumb and forefinger.
2. A touchdown is scored when a player advances the ball so that part of it is extended over the edge of the table. Also, a touchdown gets a kick for an extra point.
3. A kick is scored when the ball is held by one hand and flicked with the other hand, and travels through the goalpost formed by the finger of the opposing team.
4. If the opponent flicks the ball off the table four times, the opposing player gets to kick a field goal.

Process Questions

1. How would you define addiction?
2. How would you compare this game to addiction?
3. What are some things that may help you win?
4. What are some things that may cause you to lose?

6.3a Substance Use Disorder

Many people simply do not understand how a person can have a predisposition or develop a substance use disorder. They attribute substance use disorder to a breakdown of moral character, lack of willpower, or foolishness, and assume the user could easily stop at any time. The reality is that substance use disorder is complex, and it takes more than good intentions and a strong will to recover.

The initial decision to use drugs is voluntary for most people, but repeated use is what often leads to brain changes that challenges the user's self-control and interfere with their ability to resist the urge to use. Because of these changes, the user is highly susceptible to relapsing even after years of sobriety (Gould, 2010; Volkow et al., 2004).

SUD Symptoms

Substance use disorder represents a cluster of symptoms that indicate the individual continues using the substance despite the resulting problems of various degrees of severity. The pathological patterns of behavior related to the use of all substances can be grouped into four areas: impairment control, social impairment, risky use, and pharmacological criteria.

Instructions: Match the patterns of behavior of substance use disorder with the descriptions of the behavior by drawing line connecting the words on the left with a box on the right.

1. Impairment Control	a. A tolerance requires markedly higher doses to achieve the same desired result. b. After prolonged use, a sudden cessation can result in a variety of withdrawal symptoms.
2. Social Impairment	a. Substances used in situations that are physically hazardous. b. Continued use despite knowledge of having problems that are made worse by the substance. c. Failure to abstain despite the difficulty it causes.
3. Risky Use	a. Failure in obligations at work, school, and home. b. Continued use despite persistent or recurrent social problems due to the effects of substance. c. Important social, work, or recreational activities may be given up or reduced due to usage. d. May withdraw from family and hobbies in order to use substances.

4. Pharmacological Criteria	a. Take the substance in larger amounts or over a longer period than intended. b. Express a persistent desire to cut down or regulate the substance and report repeated unsuccessful efforts to cut down or stop. c. Spend large amounts of time searching, using, and recovering from the substance. d. Almost all daily activities revolve around the substance. e. Overwhelming cravings may occur at any time, but are likely triggered by a conditioned association with some type of internal or external trigger.

SUD Factors

There is no single factor that can predict whether a person will have an SUD. However, there are five factors that can influence substance-use disorder (see figure 6.3).

Instructions: Using the Word Bank below to fill in the blanks.

Word Bank: (Environment, Biology, Trauma, Cognition, Attachment)

1. Having an insecure _____ is caused by a mother or caregiver that was not responsive and reliable in meeting your needs in the first three months of your life. This makes gaining and maintaining social support difficult.
2. Experiencing _____ that is not resolved can result in repeated reliving of the experience and seeking relief of the symptoms through substance use.
3. _____ accounts for about half a person's risk for addiction. Having a biological parent with alcohol use disorder increases the likelihood of developing the disorder, even if adopted into a family with no alcohol use disorder.
4. A person's _____ such as certain groups are prone to alcohol use disorders, including males, people with low education and income, people who have divorced, and people in certain occupations with a drinking culture.
5. Our _____ drives the thousands of words we say to ourselves daily; this is called self-talk. Most of our self-talk is negative, which can lead to the negative behaviors of substance use.

The Cycle of Addiction

Most drugs simulate a flood of the brain's chemical messenger, dopamine, a reward center (see figure 6.3 Step1a). This reward center controls the body's ability to feel pleasure and motivates behaviors needed to thrive (e.g. eating and socializing). This overstimulation of the reward center causes the intensely pleasurable high that leads to repeated use (Gould, 2010; Volkow et al., 2004).

Continued use causes the brain to adjust to the excess dopamine by making less of it and/or reducing the ability of cells in the reward center to respond to it. This reduces the high that the person feels compared to the high they felt when first taking the drug. In other words, they become more tolerant. The reaction is taking more to obtain the same high. Additionally, it may cause less pleasure from other things previously enjoyed, like eating or social activities (Gould, 2010; Volkow et al., 2004). The user requires the substance just to feel normal and avoid feeling bad (see figure 6.3 Step 1b).

Other cues from the environment (senses, memories, places, feelings, etc.) that are associated with the high (see figure 6.3 Step 2) can trigger the craving to seek the substance, to use the substance (see figure 6.3 Step 3), and then to experience the remorse of using (see figure 6.3 Step 4) and repeat the cycle.

Process Questions:

1. How do you know if you have a substance use disorder?
2. What factors in your own life make you susceptible to addiction?
3. What makes the addiction cycle so difficult to break?

6.3 A combination of biology, environment, and developmental factors influence the risk for substance used disorder.

6.3b Preparing to Change

As covered in the first session, there are five stages that people cycle through several times before they actually make a change (Prochaska, DiClemente and Norcross, 1992). The stages are: maintenance, preparation, relapse, pre-contemplation, action, contemplation

1. **Pre-contemplation**: You do not see a need to change right now.
2. **Contemplation**: You see a need for change and are thinking about changing.
3. **Preparation**: You intend to take action in the near future.
4. **Action**: You change your behavior.
5. **Maintenance**: You need to sustain the change and not slip back into the rut.
6. **Relapse**: You begin again.

Change is not easy, and after you change, you can often fall back into old patterns, so you have to keep trying.

We Are Resistant to Change

As mentioned earlier, the concept of homeostasis is from the field of biology. The human body regulates itself to keep a steady-state of homeostasis (Cannon, 1932). An example is when our body temperature gets above 98.6, our body perspires to cool it back to equilibrium. In short, any change in the body is met with resistance, and an attempt is made to change it back.

    This concept is also used in family therapy. The idea is that families and individuals resist change to maintain the steady state. This is what keeps families and individuals stuck in cycles or behaviors. It is like a car getting stuck in a rut. The car wheel is trying to roll forward, but cannot get the momentum to break free and rolls right back into the rut.

Recognizing Our Discrepancy

People are more persuaded by what they hear themselves say than by what other people tell them. Helping the family focus attention on how current behavior differs from ideal or desired behavior is an important step in making a change. An example is: your goal or desire is to be a happy family together, but your substance use is causing the family pain and tearing it apart.

This requires listening to what the family expresses as their goals or values. You can help change the family's perception without creating a sense of being pressured or coerced. The change in the family is motivated by the perceived discrepancy between current family functioning and important family goals and values.

Finding a Support Group

Families and friends who've been affected by addiction also need comfort and support. By associating with other family members who are going through a similar situation, it helps them advance in their own recovery process. This is how emotional healing begins, and why support groups for families of drug addicts are so important.

Support groups allow members to help each other. Many of us learn the most when we teach others. For those who devote their time and energy to helping others in recovery, the emotional and psychological benefits are quite tangible. By not only receiving support, but by also giving it, a member's involvement is increased and more is gained from the experience.

While support groups for drug and alcohol abuse aren't the final answers to recovery's questions, they're extremely **beneficial to the process**. Those who participate in these groups generally have a more positive attitude towards their treatment and are better equipped to maintain sustained recovery.

Process Questions:

1. Why is change so difficult?
2. How does the stages of change model help you think about successful change?

6.3b We are resistant to change, but by recognizing how our substance use keeps us from our deepest desires or goals, and with support from others, we can change.

6.3c Step Up to Change

Motivational Interviewing (MI) is a counseling style that was initially used to treat addiction, but is increasingly being used for other social-helping professions. MI can be used to create an environment to facilitate change for a user. In MI, there are five strategies that are useful in helping to motivate change:

1. Introduce the topic with openness, concern, and lack of judgment to establish rapport

Establishing rapport with the user decreases defensiveness and increases openness to the possibility of change. Expressing acceptance and affirmation is important (Rollnick & Miller 1995).

> **Helper:** There are some signs of drug use and, because I care about your health, I'd like to explore ways I can help you. What can you tell me about your drug use?

2. Assess motivation

One method of assessing motivation is to use a scale of 1 to 10 and to ask why motivation is not *lower*:

> **Helper:** "How ready are you to quit, on a scale of 1 to 10?"
> **User:** "I'd say a 4."
> **Helper:** "Why not lower?"
> **User:** "Lower?'. . . . Why not lower? Um, well, there's my job that's important to me . . ."

Asking, "Why not *lower*?" is likely to produce some statement of motivation, whereas asking, "Why not *higher*?" is likely to produce excuses. Also, gauge the user's confidence in his/her ability to change and readiness for change (Rounsaville 2002).

3. Elicit statements of motivation

Use open-ended questioning and reflective listening to elicit the patient's own explanations for behaviors, recognition or concerns about a problem, and desire, intention, and ability to change.

For example, say:

> **Helper:** "How is your drinking affecting your life?"
> **User:** "It's ruining my marriage!"

4. Resolve ambivalence

Patients often have a high degree of ambivalence about changing their addictive behavior (Wagner & Conners 2003c); they want both the pleasures of indulgence and the benefits of restraint. Help the patient explore, articulate, and clarify ambivalence he or she may have about the problem behavior. Highlight discrepancies in what the patient says in order to produce internal tension that can lead to change.

For example, say:

> **Helper:** "From what you say, drinking is important to your social life, while at the same time, it is hurting your most important relationships. What do you think about that?"
> **User:** "Keeping my girlfriend is really more important."

5. Plan for change

In motivational interviewing, the client comes up with his or her own plan for change (Ingersoll et al. 2000; Rosengren & Wagner 2001). Elicit a plan from the patient for the next 30 to 90 days. The plan is based on the patient's current stage of change and does not need to include quitting if the patient isn't ready.

For example, ask:

> **Helper:** "What step, if any, can you do in the next month to move in the direction of thinking about quitting?"
> **User**: "I can attend a follow-up appointment."

Here are the 12 Steps as defined by Alcoholics Anonymous:

1. We admitted we were powerless over alcohol, that our lives had become unmanageable.
2. We came to believe that a Power greater than ourselves could restore us to sanity.
3. We made a decision to turn our will and our lives over to the care of God as we understood Him.

4. We made a searching and fearless moral inventory of ourselves.
5. We admitted to God, to ourselves and to another human being the exact nature of our wrongs.
6. We were entirely ready to have God remove all these defects of character
7. Humbly asked Him to remove our shortcomings
8. We made a list of persons we had harmed, and became willing to make amends to them all.
9. We made direct amends to such people wherever possible, except when to do so would injure them or others.
10. We continued to take personal inventory and, when we were wrong, promptly admitted it.
11. We sought through prayer and meditation to improve our conscious contact with God as we understood Him, praying only for knowledge of His will for us and the power to carry that out.
12. Having had a spiritual awakening as the result of these steps, we tried to carry this message to alcoholics and to practice these principles in all our affairs.

Process Questions:

1. What do you think is the key to making motivational interviewing effective?
2. What is the role of faith in recovery?

6.3c Research has shown that self-help groups such as Alcoholics Anonymous (AA) that the 12 Steps assists with long-term sobriety and recovery.

6.4 The Dad Plan

Fathering Skill: I will become a better dad; no matter how tough, I won't quit or give up, through community support of my faith, family, and community until my last breath and my eyes finally shut.

Remember to use SMART goals for your plan to turn your life around.

Instructions: Answer the following questions to create your dad plan to become a better dad.

1. What is my specific SMART (Specific, Measurable, Achievable, Realistic, Timetable) goal for growing in cultural awareness?

2. What can I do every day this week to grow more culturally aware?

3. When and where will I do this?

4. Who will hold me accountable?

7.0 References

Bowlby, J. (1969), *Attachment and loss, Vol. 1: Attachment.* New York: Basic Books.

Epstein, N., Bishop, D., & Baldwin, L. (1984). McMaster model of family functioning. In D. H. Olson, & P. M. Miller (Eds.), Family studies review year-book (Vol. 2). New Delhi: Sage Publications

Gould, T. J. (2010). Addiction and cognition, *Addiction Science Clinical Practice, 5(2),* 4-14.

Henriques, G. (2013). On making judgments and being judgmental: Eight dynamics to consider in making constructive judgments. Psychology Today. Retrieved from: https://www.psychologytoday.com/blog/theory-knowledge/201305/making-judgments-and-being-judgmental

Henriques, D. (2014). The Core Need. Psychology Today. Retrieved from https://www.psychologytoday.com/blog/theory-knowledge/201406/the-core-need

Hibel, James, "Cooperation And Competition In Family, Pseudo-Family And Peer Triads" (1981). *Child and Family Studies—Dissertations.* 54.

https://surface.syr.edu/cfs_etd/54

National Association of Social Workers. (2008). *Code of ethics of the National Association of Social Workers.* Washington, DC: NASW Press.

Prentice, R. (2014). Teaching behavioral ethics. Journal of Legal Studies Education, 31(2), 325-365.

Van der Kolk, B. A. (2014). *The body keeps the score: Brain, mind, and body in the healing of trauma.* New York: VikingU.S. Census. (2015). American Indian and Alaska Native Heritage Month: November 2015. Retrieved from https://www.census.gov/newsroom/facts-for-features/2015/cb15-ff22.html

Rycus, J. S. (1998). The field guide to child welfare volume III: Child development and child welfare, Child Welfare League of America Press.

Genovese, E. (1976). "The Political Crisis of Social History: A Marxian Perspective", Journal of Social History, 10(2), 205–220.

Seligman, M. E., & Maier, S. F. (1967). Failure to escape traumatic shock. *Journal of Experimental Psychology, 74(1),* 1-9.

www.ingramcontent.com/pod-product-compliance
Lightning Source LLC
Chambersburg PA
CBHW081751100526
44592CB00015B/2390